MznLnx

Missing Links Exam Preps

Exam Prep for

The Economic Way of Thinking

Heyne, Boettke, Prychitko, 11th Edition

The MznLnx Exam Prep is your link from the texbook and lecture to your exams.
The MznLnx Exam Preps are unauthorized and comprehensive reviews of your textbooks.

All material provided by MznLnx and Rico Publications (c) 2010
Textbook publishers and textbook authors do not particpate in or contribute to these reviews.

MznLnx

Rico Publications

Exam Prep for The Economic Way of Thinking
11th Edition
Heyne, Boettke, Prychitko

Publisher: Raymond Houge
Assistant Editor: Michael Rouger
Text and Cover Designer: Lisa Buckner
Marketing Manager: Sara Swagger
Project Manager, Editorial Production: Jerry Emerson
Art Director: Vernon Lowerui

Product Manager: Dave Mason
Editorial Assitant: Rachel Guzmanji
Pedagogy: Debra Long
Cover Image: Jim Reed/Getty Images
Text and Cover Printer: City Printing, Inc.
Compositor: Media Mix, Inc.

(c) 2010 Rico Publications
ALL RIGHTS RESERVED. No part of this work covered by the copyright may be reproduced or used in any form or by an means--graphic, electronic, or mechanical, including photocopying, recording, taping, Web distribution, information storage, and retrieval systems, or in any other manner--without the written permission of the publisher.

Printed in the United States
ISBN:

For more information about our products, contact us at:
Dave.Mason@RicoPublications.com

For permission to use material from this text or product, submit a request online to:
Dave.Mason@RicoPublications.com

Contents

CHAPTER 1
THE ECONOMIC WAY OF THINKING   1

CHAPTER 2
EFFICIENTY, EXCHANGE, AND COMPARATIVE ADVANTAGE   8

CHAPTER 3
SUBSTITUTES EVERYWHERE: THE CONCEPT OF DEMAND   18

CHAPTER 4
OPPORTUNITY COST AND THE SUPPLY OF GOODS   25

CHAPTER 5
SUPPLY AND DEMAND: A PROCESS OF COOPERATION   28

CHAPTER 6
SUPPLY AND DEMAND: ISSUES AND APPLICATIONS   37

CHAPTER 7
PROFIT AND LOSS   44

CHAPTER 8
COMPETITION AND MONOPOLY   60

CHAPTER 9
PRICE SEARCHING   65

CHAPTER 10
COMPETITION AND GOVERNMENT POLICY   68

CHAPTER 11
THE DISTRIBUTION OF INCOME   76

CHAPTER 12
EXTERNALITIES AND CONFLICTING RIGHTS   84

CHAPTER 13
MARKETS AND GOVERNMENT   90

CHAPTER 14
THE OVERALL PERFORMANCE OF ECONOMIC SYSTEMS   99

CHAPTER 15
EMPLOYMENT AND UNEMPLOYMENT   109

CHAPTER 16
THE SUPPLY OF MONEY   115

CHAPTER 17
MONETARY AND FISCAL POLICIES   123

CHAPTER 18
ECONOMIC PERFORMANCE AND POLITICAL ECONOMY   133

CHAPTER 19
NATIONAL POLICIES AND INTERNATIONAL EXCHANGE   140

CHAPTER 20
PROMOTING ECONOMIC GROWTH   150

Contents (Cont.)

CHAPTER 21
  THE LIMITATIONS OF ECONOMICS   159
ANSWER KEY   161

TO THE STUDENT

COMPREHENSIVE

The *MznLnx* Exam Prep series is designed to help you pass your exams. Editors at MznLnx review your textbooks and then prepare these practice exams to help you master the textbook material. Unlike study guides, workbooks, and practice tests provided by the texbook publisher and textbook authors, *MznLnx* gives you **all** of the material in each chapter in exam form, not just samples, so you can be sure to nail your exam.

MECHANICAL

The MznLnx Exam Prep series creates exams that will help you learn the subject matter as well as test you on your understanding. Each question is designed to help you master the concept. Just working through the exams, you gain an understanding of the subject--its a simple mechanical process that produces success.

INTEGRATED STUDY GUIDE AND REVIEW

MznLnx is not just a set of exams designed to test you, its also a comprehensive review of the subject content. Each exam question is also a review of the concept, making sure that you will get the answer correct without having to go to other sources of material. You learn as you go! Its the easiest way to pass an exam.

HUMOR

Studying can be tedious and dry. MznLnx's instructional design includes moderate humor within the exam questions on occassion, to break the tedium and revitalize the brain

Chapter 1. THE ECONOMIC WAY OF THINKING

1. _____ is a broad label that refers to any individuals or households that use goods and services generated within the economy. The concept of a _____ is used in different contexts, so that the usage and significance of the term may vary.

Typically when business people and economists talk of _____s they are talking about person as _____, an aggregated commodity item with little individuality other than that expressed in the buy/not-buy decision.

   a. 130-30 fund
   b. Consumer
   c. 1921 recession
   d. 100-year flood

2. A _____ is a measure of the average price of consumer goods and services purchased by households. A _____ measures a price change for a constant market basket of goods and services from one period to the next within the same area (city, region, or nation.) It is a price index determined by measuring the price of a standard group of goods meant to represent the typical market basket of a typical urban consumer.
   a. CPI
   b. Lipstick index
   c. Cost-of-living index
   d. Consumer Price Index

3. In economics, the _____ is the term used to refer to the environment in which bonds are bought and sold between a central bank ' its regulated banks. It is not a free market process.

- To intervene in the 'business cycle', a central bank may choose to go into the _____ and buy or sell government bonds, which is known as _____ operations to increase reserves.

   a. Inside money
   b. Outside money
   c. Open Market
   d. ACCRA Cost of Living Index

4. _____ in economics and business is the result of an exchange and from that trade we assign a numerical monetary value to a good, service or asset. If Alice trades Bob 4 apples for an orange, the _____ of an orange is 4 apples. Inversely, the _____ of an apple is 1/4 oranges.
   a. Price book
   b. Price
   c. Premium pricing
   d. Price war

5. A _____ is a normalized average (typically a weighted average) of prices for a given class of goods or services in a given region, during a given interval of time. It is a statistic designed to help to compare how these prices, taken as a whole, differ between time periods or geographical locations.

Price indices have several potential uses.

   a. Two-part tariff
   b. Price Index
   c. Transactional Net Margin Method
   d. Product sabotage

6. _____s is the social science that studies the production, distribution, and consumption of goods and services. The term _____s comes from the Ancient Greek oá¼°κονομῖα from oá¼¶κος (oikos, 'house') + vÏŒμος (nomos, 'custom' or 'law'), hence 'rules of the house(hold)'. Current _____ models developed out of the broader field of political economy in the late 19th century, owing to a desire to use an empirical approach more akin to the physical sciences.

Chapter 1. THE ECONOMIC WAY OF THINKING

a. Energy economics
b. Inflation
c. Opportunity cost
d. Economic

7. _____ is a term used in economic research and policy debates. As with freedom generally, there are various definitions, but no universally accepted concept of _____. One major approach to _____ comes from the libertarian tradition emphasizing free markets and private property, while another extends the welfare economics study of individual choice, with greater _____ coming from a 'larger' (in some technical sense) set of possible choices.

a. Economic liberalization
b. International sanctions
c. Investment policy
d. Economic Freedom

8. A _____ occurs when an entity spends more money than it takes in. The opposite of a _____ is a budget surplus. Debt is essentially an accumulated flow of deficits.

a. Lump-sum tax
b. Public Financial Management
c. Funding body
d. Budget deficit

9. A _____ is an object whose consumption increases the utility of the consumer, for which the quantity demanded exceeds the quantity supplied at zero price. _____s are usually modeled as having diminishing marginal utility. The first individual purchase has high utility; the second has less.

a. Pie method
b. Composite good
c. Good
d. Merit good

10. _____ was a survey conducted by the U.S. Department of Justice to gauge the prevalence of alcohol and illegal drug use among prior arrestees. It was a reformulation of the prior Drug Use Forecasting (DUF) program, focused on five drugs in particular: cocaine, marijuana, methamphetamine, opiates, and PCP.

Participants were randomly selected from arrest records in major metropolitan areas; because no personally identifying information is taken from each record chosen, the resulting data can be correlated to arrest rates, but not to the total population of persons charged.

a. ACEA agreement
b. AD-IA Model
c. Arrestee Drug Abuse Monitoring
d. ACCRA Cost of Living Index

11. Necessary _____s:

If x is a necessary _____ of y, then the presence of y necessarily implies the presence of x. The presence of x, however, does not imply that y will occur.

Sufficient _____s:

If x is a sufficient _____ of y, then the presence of x necessarily implies the presence of y.

a. Political philosophy
b. Philosophy of economics
c. Materialism
d. Cause

Chapter 1. THE ECONOMIC WAY OF THINKING

12. An _____ is the magnum opus of the Scottish economist Adam Smith. It is a clearly written account of economics at the dawn of the Industrial Revolution, as well as a rhetorical piece written for the generally educated individual of the 18th century - advocating a free market economy as more productive and more beneficial to society.

The work is credited as a watershed in history and economics due to its comprehensive, largely accurate characterization of economic mechanisms that survive in modern economics; and also for its effective use of rhetorical technique, including structuring the work to contrast real world examples of free and fettered markets.

   a. AD-IA Model
   b. ACCRA Cost of Living Index
   c. ACEA agreement
   d. Inquiry into the Nature and Causes of the Wealth of Nations

13. _____ was a Scottish moral philosopher and a pioneer of political economy. One of the key figures of the Scottish Enlightenment, Smith is the author of The Theory of Moral Sentiments and An Inquiry into the Nature and Causes of the Wealth of Nations. The latter, usually abbreviated as The Wealth of Nations, is considered his magnum opus and the first modern work of economics.

   a. Adam Smith
   b. Adolph Fischer
   c. Adolf Hitler
   d. Alan Greenspan

14. An Inquiry into the Nature and Causes of the _____ is the magnum opus of the Scottish economist Adam Smith. It is a clearly written account of economics at the dawn of the Industrial Revolution, as well as a rhetorical piece written for the generally educated individual of the 18th century - advocating a free market economy as more productive and more beneficial to society.

The work is credited as a watershed in history and economics due to its comprehensive, largely accurate characterization of economic mechanisms that survive in modern economics; and also for its effective use of rhetorical technique, including structuring the work to contrast real world examples of free and fettered markets.

   a. Black Book of Communism
   b. The Rise and Fall of the Great Powers
   c. The Bell Curve
   d. Wealth of Nations

15. An Inquiry into the Nature and Causes of _____ is the magnum opus of the Scottish economist Adam Smith. It is a clearly written account of economics at the dawn of the Industrial Revolution, as well as a rhetorical piece written for the generally educated individual of the 18th century - advocating a free market economy as more productive and more beneficial to society.

The work is credited as a watershed in history and economics due to its comprehensive, largely accurate characterization of economic mechanisms that survive in modern economics; and also for its effective use of rhetorical technique, including structuring the work to contrast real world examples of free and fettered markets.

   a. Banks and Politics in America
   b. The Rise and Fall of the Great Powers
   c. Capital and Interest
   d. The Wealth of Nations

Chapter 1. THE ECONOMIC WAY OF THINKING

16. _____ is a term used to collectively describe topics relating to the operations of firms with interests in multiple countries. Such firms are sometimes called multinational corporations . Well known MNCs include fast food companies McDonald's and Yum Brands, vehicle manufacturers such as General Motors and Toyota, consumer electronics companies like Samsung, LG and Sony, and energy companies such as ExxonMobil and BP.

   a. ACEA agreement
   b. ACCRA Cost of Living Index
   c. AD-IA Model
   d. International Business

17. _____, 1st Baron Keynes was a renowned economist from Britain whose many ideas on economic and political theories as well as on many governments' monetary policies influenced America. He advocated a government that played an active role in the lives of people regarding business, economy, etc. In this role, the government would use fiscal measures to reduce the consequences of recessions, economic depressions and booms.

   a. Adam Smith
   b. Adolph Fischer
   c. Adolf Hitler
   d. John Maynard Keynes

18. _____ is an online peer-reviewed magazine published by the Agricultural ' Applied Economics Association (AAEA) for readers interested in the policy and management of agriculture, the food industry, natural resources, rural communities, and the environment. _____ is published quarterly and is available free online. It is currently one of three outreach products offered by AAEA, along with the more timely Policy Issues and the forthcoming Shared Materials section of the AAEA Web site.

   a. 100-year flood
   b. 1921 recession
   c. 130-30 fund
   d. Choices

19. _____, or a _____ is the concept of a resulting effect (cf. cause and effect, arising from another action. In general terms, it is used to indicate that all human actions, particularly crime and sin, have profound effects.

   a. Variability
   b. Rule
   c. Solved
   d. Consequence

20. _____ refers to the state of not requiring any outside aid, support for survival; it is therefore a type of personal or collective autonomy. On a large scale, a totally self-sufficient economy that does not trade with the outside world is called an autarky.

The term _____ is usually applied to varieties of sustainable living in which nothing is consumed outside of what is produced by the self-sufficient individuals.

   a. Sustainable forest management
   b. Global Reporting Initiative
   c. Sustainability science
   d. Self-sufficiency

21. A _____ is a situation that involves losing one quality or aspect of something in return for gaining another quality or aspect. It implies a decision to be made with full comprehension of both the upside and downside of a particular choice.

In economics the term is expressed as opportunity cost, referring the most preferred alternative given up.

   a. Trade-off
   b. Whitemail
   c. Nonmarket
   d. Friedman-Savage utility function

Chapter 1. THE ECONOMIC WAY OF THINKING

22. In finance, the term _____ describes various legal measures taken to ensure that debtors, whether individuals, businesses honor their debts and make an honest effort to repay the money that they owe. Generally regarded as a subdivision of tax law, _____ is most often enforced through a combination of audits and legal restrictions. For example, a provision of the Federal Debt Collection Procedure Act states that a person or organization indebted to the United States, against whom a judgment lien has been filed, is ineligible to receive a government grant.
    a. Carryback loan
    b. Debt compliance
    c. Microcredit
    d. Hard money loan

23. In economics and sociology, an _____ is any factor (financial or non-financial) that enables or motivates a particular course of action, or counts as a reason for preferring one choice to the alternatives. It is an expectation that encourages people to behave in a certain way. Since human beings are purposeful creatures, the study of _____ structures is central to the study of all economic activity (both in terms of individual decision-making and in terms of co-operation and competition within a larger institutional structure.)
    a. Epstein-Zin preferences
    b. Economic reform
    c. Incentive
    d. Isocost

Chapter 1. THE ECONOMIC WAY OF THINKING

24. A _____ is:

- Rewrite _____, in generative grammar and computer science
- Standardization, a formal and widely-accepted statement, fact, definition, or qualification
- Operation, a determinate _____ for performing a mathematical operation and obtaining a certain result (Mathematics, Logic)
    - Unary operation
    - Binary operation
- _____ of inference, a function from sets of formulae to formulae (Mathematics, Logic)
- _____ of thumb, principle with broad application that is not intended to be strictly accurate or reliable for every situation. Also often simply referred to as a _____
- Moral, an atomic element of a moral code for guiding choices in human behavior
- Heuristic, a quantized '_____' which shows a tendency or probability for successful function
- A regulation, as in sports
- A Production _____, as in computer science
- Procedural law, a _____ set governing the application of laws to cases
    - A law, which may informally be called a '_____'
    - A court ruling, a decision by a court
- In the U.S. Government, a regulation mandated by Congress, but written or expanded upon by the Executive Branch.
- Norm (sociology), an informal but widely accepted _____, concept, truth, definition, or qualification (social norms, legal norms, coding norms)
- Norm (philosophy), a kind of sentence or a reason to act, feel or believe
- 'Rulership' is the concept of governance by a government:
    - Military _____, governance by a military body
    - Monastic _____, a collection of precepts that guides the life of monks or nuns in a religious order where the superior holds the place of Christ
- Slide _____

- '_____,' a song by Ayumi Hamasaki
- '_____,' a song by rapper Nas
- '_____s,' an album by the band The Whitest Boy Alive
- _____s: Pyaar Ka Superhit Formula, a 2003 Bollywood film
- ruler, an instrument for measuring lengths
- _____, a component of an astrolabe, circumferator or similar instrument
- The _____s, a bestselling self-help book
- _____ Project (Run Up-to-date Linux Everywhere), a project that aims to use up-to-date Linux software on old PCs
- _____ engine, a software system that helps managing business _____s
- Ja _____, a hip hop artist
    - R.U.L.E., a 2005 greatest hits album by rapper Ja _____
- '_____s,' a KMFDM song

a. Procter ' Gamble
b. Rule
c. Demand
d. Technocracy

25. _____ is a fee paid on borrowed assets. It is the price paid for the use of borrowed money, or, money earned by deposited funds. Assets that are sometimes lent with _____ include money, shares, consumer goods through hire purchase, major assets such as aircraft, and even entire factories in finance lease arrangements.

a. Interest
b. Internal debt
c. Insolvency
d. Asset protection

26. A _____ is the exclusive authority to determine how a resource is used, whether that resource is owned by government or by individuals. All economic goods have a _____s attribute. This attribute has three broad components

1. The right to use the good
2. The right to earn income from the good
3. The right to transfer the good to others

The concept of _____s as used by economists and legal scholars are related but distinct. The distinction is largely seen in the economists' focus on the ability of an individual or collective to control the use of the good.

a. Property right
b. High-reeve
c. Post-sale restraint
d. Holder in due course

27. _____ is a term used to described a tendency or preference towards a particular perspective, ideology or result, especially when the tendency interferes with the ability to be impartial, unprejudiced, or objective. The term _____ed is used to describe an action, judgment, or other outcome influenced by a prejudged perspective. It is also used to refer to a person or body of people whose actions or judgments exhibit _____.

a. Bias
b. 100-year flood
c. 1921 recession
d. 130-30 fund

28. The _____ is one of several stock market indices, created by nineteenth-century Wall Street Journal editor and Dow Jones' Company co-founder Charles Dow. It is an index that shows how certain stocks have traded. Dow compiled the index to gauge the performance of the industrial sector of the American stock market.

a. Fama-French three factor model
b. Commodity fetishism
c. Federal Reserve Bank Notes
d. Dow Jones Industrial Average

Chapter 2. EFFICIENTY, EXCHANGE, AND COMPARATIVE ADVANTAGE

1. A _____ occurs when an entity spends more money than it takes in. The opposite of a _____ is a budget surplus. Debt is essentially an accumulated flow of deficits.
   a. Public Financial Management
   b. Lump-sum tax
   c. Funding body
   d. Budget deficit

2. _____ is a type of trade policy that allows traders to act and transact without interference from government. Thus, the policy permits trading partners mutual gains from trade, with goods and services produced according to the theory of comparative advantage.

   Under a _____ policy, prices are a reflection of true supply and demand, and are the sole determinant of resource allocation.

   a. 1921 recession
   b. 130-30 fund
   c. Free trade
   d. 100-year flood

3. A _____ is any systematic process enabling many market players to bid and ask: helping bidders and sellers interact and make deals. It is not just the price mechanism but the entire system of regulation, qualification, credentials, reputations and clearing that surrounds that mechanism and makes it operate in a social context.

   Because a _____ relies on the assumption that players are constantly involved and unequally enabled, a _____ is distinguished specifically from a voting system where candidates seek the support of voters on a less regular basis.

   a. Contestable market
   b. Market system
   c. Competitive equilibrium
   d. Price mechanism

4. The _____ is a term used in economics to describe a good that is not scarce. A _____ is available in as great a quantity as desired with zero opportunity cost to society.

   A good that is made available at zero price is not necessarily a _____.

   a. Free good
   b. Giffen good
   c. Durable good
   d. Merit good

5. A _____ is an object whose consumption increases the utility of the consumer, for which the quantity demanded exceeds the quantity supplied at zero price. _____s are usually modeled as having diminishing marginal utility. The first individual purchase has high utility; the second has less.
   a. Pie method
   b. Composite good
   c. Merit good
   d. Good

6. _____ is a fee paid on borrowed assets. It is the price paid for the use of borrowed money, or, money earned by deposited funds. Assets that are sometimes lent with _____ include money, shares, consumer goods through hire purchase, major assets such as aircraft, and even entire factories in finance lease arrangements.
   a. Asset protection
   b. Insolvency
   c. Internal debt
   d. Interest

Chapter 2. EFFICIENTY, EXCHANGE, AND COMPARATIVE ADVANTAGE

7. A _____ is the exclusive authority to determine how a resource is used, whether that resource is owned by government or by individuals. All economic goods have a _____s attribute. This attribute has three broad components

   1. The right to use the good
   2. The right to earn income from the good
   3. The right to transfer the good to others

The concept of _____s as used by economists and legal scholars are related but distinct. The distinction is largely seen in the economists' focus on the ability of an individual or collective to control the use of the good.

   a. Post-sale restraint
   b. High-reeve
   c. Holder in due course
   d. Property right

8. _____s is the social science that studies the production, distribution, and consumption of goods and services. The term _____s comes from the Ancient Greek oá¼°κονομῖα from oá¼¶κος (oikos, 'house') + vĭŒμος (nomos, 'custom' or 'law'), hence 'rules of the house(hold)'. Current _____ models developed out of the broader field of political economy in the late 19th century, owing to a desire to use an empirical approach more akin to the physical sciences.
   a. Energy economics
   b. Opportunity cost
   c. Inflation
   d. Economic

9. _____ is a term used in economic research and policy debates. As with freedom generally, there are various definitions, but no universally accepted concept of _____. One major approach to _____ comes from the libertarian tradition emphasizing free markets and private property, while another extends the welfare economics study of individual choice, with greater _____ coming from a 'larger' (in some technical sense) set of possible choices.
   a. International sanctions
   b. Economic liberalization
   c. Economic Freedom
   d. Investment policy

10. _____ is the political philosophy and practice derived from the work of Karl Marx and Friedrich Engels. _____ holds at its core a critical analysis of capitalism and a theory of social change. The powerful and innovative methods of analysis introduced by Marx have been very influential in a broad range of disciplines.
    a. Adam Smith
    b. Karl Heinrich Marx
    c. Marxism
    d. Neo-Gramscianism

11. _____ was the theoretical journal of the Communist Party of Great Britain and was dissolved in 1991. It was particularly important during the 1980s under the editorship of Martin Jacques. Through _____ Jacques, amongst others, coined the term Thatcherism and believed they were deconstructing the ideology of the government of the then Prime Minister of the United Kingdom, Margaret Thatcher, through their theory of New Times.
    a. 130-30 fund
    b. 100-year flood
    c. Marxism Today
    d. 1921 recession

12. _____ is the increase in the amount of the goods and services produced by an economy over time. It is conventionally measured as the percent rate of increase in real gross domestic product, or real GDP. Growth is usually calculated in real terms, i.e. inflation-adjusted terms, in order to net out the effect of inflation on the price of the goods and services produced.

Chapter 2. EFFICIENTY, EXCHANGE, AND COMPARATIVE ADVANTAGE

a. ACEA agreement
b. Economic growth
c. ACCRA Cost of Living Index
d. AD-IA Model

13. _____ was a survey conducted by the U.S. Department of Justice to gauge the prevalence of alcohol and illegal drug use among prior arrestees. It was a reformulation of the prior Drug Use Forecasting (DUF) program, focused on five drugs in particular: cocaine, marijuana, methamphetamine, opiates, and PCP.

Participants were randomly selected from arrest records in major metropolitan areas; because no personally identifying information is taken from each record chosen, the resulting data can be correlated to arrest rates, but not to the total population of persons charged.

a. ACCRA Cost of Living Index
b. ACEA agreement
c. AD-IA Model
d. Arrestee Drug Abuse Monitoring

14. _____ is sometimes referred to as _____, actually it means Economic Monetary Union.

First ideas of an economic and monetary union in Europe were raised well before establishing the European Communities. For example, already in the League of Nations, Gustav Stresemann asked in 1929 for a European currency (Link) against the background of an increased economic division due to a number of new nation states in Europe after WWI.

a. Exchange rate mechanism
b. European Monetary System
c. Euro Interbank Offered Rate
d. European Monetary Union

15. An economic and _____ is a single market with a common currency. It is to be distinguished from a mere currency union, which does not involve a single market. This is the fifth stage of economic integration.

a. Commercial invoice
b. Customs union
c. Monetary Union
d. Free trade zone

16. _____ was a Scottish moral philosopher and a pioneer of political economy. One of the key figures of the Scottish Enlightenment, Smith is the author of The Theory of Moral Sentiments and An Inquiry into the Nature and Causes of the Wealth of Nations. The latter, usually abbreviated as The Wealth of Nations, is considered his magnum opus and the first modern work of economics.

a. Adolph Fischer
b. Adolf Hitler
c. Alan Greenspan
d. Adam Smith

17. The _____ consists of a number of economic theories which describe the nature of the firm, company including its existence, its behaviour, and its relationship with the market.

Chapter 2. EFFICIENTY, EXCHANGE, AND COMPARATIVE ADVANTAGE

In simplified terms, the _____ aims to answer these questions:

1. Existence - why do firms emerge, why are not all transactions in the economy mediated over the market?
2. Boundaries - why the boundary between firms and the market is located exactly there? Which transactions are performed internally and which are negotiated on the market?
3. Organization - why are firms structured in such specific way? What is the interplay of formal and informal relationships?

Despite looking simple, these questions are not answered by the established economic theory, which usually views firms as given, and treats them as black boxes without any internal structure.

The First World War period saw a change of emphasis in economic theory away from industry-level analysis which mainly included analysing markets to analysis at the level of the firm, as it became increasingly clear that perfect competition was no longer an adequate model of how firms behaved. Economic theory till then had focussed on trying to understand markets alone and there had been little study on understanding why firms or organisations exist.

a. Technology gap
c. Policy Ineffectiveness Proposition
b. Khazzoom-Brookes postulate
d. Theory of the firm

18. _____ is the a method of technical and economic research of the systems for purpose to optimize a parity between system's consumer functions or properties and expenses to achieve those functions or properties.

This methodology for continuous perfection of production, industrial technologies, organizational structures was developed by Juryj Sobolev in 1948 at the 'Perm telephone factory'

- 1948 Juryj Sobolev - the first success in application of a method analysis at the 'Perm telephone factory'.
- 1949 - the first application for the invention as result of use of the new method.

Today in economically developed countries practically each enterprise or the company use methodology of the kind of functional-cost analysis as a practice of the quality management, most full satisfying to principles of standards of series ISO 9000.

- Interest of consumer not in products itself, but the advantage which it will receive from its usage.
- The consumer aspires to reduce his expenses
- Functions needed by consumer can be executed in the various ways, and, hence, with various efficiency and expenses. Among possible alternatives of realization of functions exist such in which the parity of quality and the price is the optimal for the consumer.

The goal of _____ is achievement of the highest consumer satisfaction of production at simultaneous decrease in all kinds of industrial expenses Classical _____ has three English synonyms - Value Engineering, Value Management, Value Analysis.

Chapter 2. EFFICIENTY, EXCHANGE, AND COMPARATIVE ADVANTAGE

a. Function cost analysis
b. Staple financing
c. Willingness to pay
d. Monopoly wage

19. _____ is used to refer to a number of related concepts. It is the using resources in such a way as to maximize the production of goods and services. A system can be called economically efficient if:

- No one can be made better off without making someone else worse off.
- More output cannot be obtained without increasing the amount of inputs.
- Production proceeds at the lowest possible per-unit cost.

These definitions of efficiency are not equivalent, but they are all encompassed by the idea that nothing more can be achieved given the resources available.

An economic system is more efficient if it can provide more goods and services for society without using more resources.

a. ACCRA Cost of Living Index
b. ACEA agreement
c. Efficient contract theory
d. Economic efficiency

20. In economics, the _____ is the term used to refer to the environment in which bonds are bought and sold between a central bank ' its regulated banks. It is not a free market process.

- To intervene in the 'business cycle', a central bank may choose to go into the _____ and buy or sell government bonds, which is known as _____ operations to increase reserves.

a. ACCRA Cost of Living Index
b. Open Market
c. Outside money
d. Inside money

21. _____ or economic opportunity loss is the value of the next best alternative foregone as the result of making a decision. _____ analysis is an important part of a company's decision-making processes but is not treated as an actual cost in any financial statement. The next best thing that a person can engage in is referred to as the _____ of doing the best thing and ignoring the next best thing to be done.

a. Industrial organization
b. Economic ideology
c. Economic
d. Opportunity cost

22. In microeconomics, _____ is quite simply the conversion of inputs into outputs. It is an economic process that uses resources to create a good or service that is suitable for exchange. This can include manufacturing, storing, shipping, and packaging.

a. MET
b. Production
c. Red Guards
d. Solved

23. _____ originally was the term for studying production, buying and selling, and their relations with law, custom, and government. _____ originated in moral philosophy. It developed in the 18th century as the study of the economies of states -- polities, hence _____.

Chapter 2. EFFICIENTY, EXCHANGE, AND COMPARATIVE ADVANTAGE

a. Dirigisme
b. Productive and unproductive labour
c. Geoeconomics
d. Political Economy

24. _____ by John Stuart Mill was the most important economics or political economy textbook of the mid nineteenth century. It was revised until its seventh edition in 1871, shortly before Mill's death in 1873, and republished in numerous other editions.

Mill's Principles were written in a style of prose far flung from the introductory texts of today.

a. Limits to Growth
b. Principles of Political Economy and Taxation
c. The Rise and Fall of the Great Powers
d. Principles of Political Economy

25. On the _____ is a book by David Ricardo on economics. The book concludes that land rent grows as population increases. It also clearly lays out the theory of comparative advantage, which shows that all nations can benefit from free trade, even if a nation lacks an absolute advantage in all sectors of its economy.

a. Principles of Political Economy and Taxation
b. The Wealth of Nations
c. Butterfly Economics
d. Theory of Moral Sentiments

26. In economics, _____ refers to the ability of a person or a country to produce a particular good at a lower marginal cost and opportunity cost than another person or country. It is the ability to produce a product most efficiently given all the other products that could be produced. It can be contrasted with absolute advantage which refers to the ability of a person or a country to produce a particular good at a lower absolute cost than another.

a. Gravity model of trade
b. Comparative advantage
c. Hot money
d. Triffin dilemma

27. In economics, the _____ is the idea that a nation is better off when it produces goods and services for which it has a comparative advantage.

a. Recession
b. Keynesian economics
c. Law of comparative advantage
d. Monopolistic competition

28. _____ is a broad label that refers to any individuals or households that use goods and services generated within the economy. The concept of a _____ is used in different contexts, so that the usage and significance of the term may vary.

Typically when business people and economists talk of _____s they are talking about person as _____, an aggregated commodity item with little individuality other than that expressed in the buy/not-buy decision.

a. 100-year flood
b. 130-30 fund
c. 1921 recession
d. Consumer

29. A _____ is a measure of the average price of consumer goods and services purchased by households. A _____ measures a price change for a constant market basket of goods and services from one period to the next within the same area (city, region, or nation.) It is a price index determined by measuring the price of a standard group of goods meant to represent the typical market basket of a typical urban consumer.

a. Cost-of-living index
c. Lipstick index
b. CPI
d. Consumer Price Index

30. _____ in economics and business is the result of an exchange and from that trade we assign a numerical monetary value to a good, service or asset. If Alice trades Bob 4 apples for an orange, the _____ of an orange is 4 apples. Inversely, the _____ of an apple is 1/4 oranges.
   a. Price book
   b. Price war
   c. Premium pricing
   d. Price

31. A _____ is a normalized average (typically a weighted average) of prices for a given class of goods or services in a given region, during a given interval of time. It is a statistic designed to help to compare how these prices, taken as a whole, differ between time periods or geographical locations.

Price indices have several potential uses.

   a. Product sabotage
   b. Two-part tariff
   c. Transactional Net Margin Method
   d. Price Index

32. In economics and related disciplines, a _____ is a cost incurred in making an economic exchange. For example, most people, when buying or selling a stock, must pay a commission to their broker; that commission is a _____ of doing the stock deal. Or consider buying a banana from a store; to purchase the banana, your costs will be not only the price of the banana itself, but also the energy and effort it requires to find out which of the various banana products you prefer, where to get them and at what price, the cost of traveling from your house to the store and back, the time waiting in line, and the effort of the paying itself; the costs above and beyond the cost of the banana are the _____s.
   a. Cost of poor quality
   b. Transaction cost
   c. Sliding scale fees
   d. Cost allocation

33. The _____ is a group of three respected economists who advise the President of the United States on economic policy. It is a part of the Executive Office of the President of the United States, and provides much of the economic policy of the White House. The council prepares the annual Economic Report of the President.
   a. Constrained Pareto optimality
   b. Hybrid renewable energy systems
   c. Federal Reserve Bank Notes
   d. Council of Economic Advisers

34. In economics and sociology, an _____ is any factor (financial or non-financial) that enables or motivates a particular course of action, or counts as a reason for preferring one choice to the alternatives. It is an expectation that encourages people to behave in a certain way. Since human beings are purposeful creatures, the study of _____ structures is central to the study of all economic activity (both in terms of individual decision-making and in terms of co-operation and competition within a larger institutional structure.)
   a. Epstein-Zin preferences
   b. Economic reform
   c. Isocost
   d. Incentive

35. _____ is a term that encompasses the notion of individuals and firms striving for a greater share of a market to sell or buy goods and services. Merriam-Webster defines competition in business as 'the effort of two or more parties acting independently to secure the business of a third party by offering the most favorable terms.' It was described by Adam Smith in The Wealth of Nations (1776) and later economists as allocating productive resources to their most highly-valued uses. and encouraging efficiency.

Chapter 2. EFFICIENTY, EXCHANGE, AND COMPARATIVE ADVANTAGE

a. Competition in economics
b. Moral victory
c. Price fixing
d. Strategic entry deterrence

36. The _____ was an early English joint-stock company that was formed initially for pursuing trade with the East Indies, but that ended up trading with the Indian subcontinent and China. The oldest among several similarly formed European East India Companies, the Company was granted an English Royal Charter, under the name Governor and Company of Merchants of London Trading into the East Indies, by Elizabeth I on 31 December 1600. After a rival English company challenged its monopoly in the late 17th century, the two companies were merged in 1708 to form the United Company of Merchants of England Trading to the East Indies, commonly styled the Honourable _____, and abbreviated, HEast India Company; the Company was colloquially referred to as John Company, and in India as Company Bahadur .

a. ACEA agreement
b. AD-IA Model
c. East India Company
d. ACCRA Cost of Living Index

37. In economics, the _____ is a historical inverse relation between the rate of unemployment and the rate of inflation in an economy. Stated simply, the lower the unemployment in an economy, the higher the rate of increase in nominal wages in the economy. Rate of Change of Wages against Unemployment, United Kingdom 1913-1948 from Phillips (1958)

William Phillips, a New Zealand born economist, wrote a paper in 1958 titled The Relationship between Unemployment and the Rate of Change of Money Wages in the United Kingdom 1861-1957, which was published in the quarterly journal Economica.

a. Lorenz curve
b. Phillips curve
c. Demand curve
d. Cost curve

38. In finance, the term _____ describes various legal measures taken to ensure that debtors, whether individuals, businesses honor their debts and make an honest effort to repay the money that they owe. Generally regarded as a subdivision of tax law, _____ is most often enforced through a combination of audits and legal restrictions. For example, a provision of the Federal Debt Collection Procedure Act states that a person or organization indebted to the United States, against whom a judgment lien has been filed, is ineligible to receive a government grant.

a. Carryback loan
b. Hard money loan
c. Debt compliance
d. Microcredit

39. An Inquiry into the Nature and Causes of the _____ is the magnum opus of the Scottish economist Adam Smith. It is a clearly written account of economics at the dawn of the Industrial Revolution, as well as a rhetorical piece written for the generally educated individual of the 18th century - advocating a free market economy as more productive and more beneficial to society.

The work is credited as a watershed in history and economics due to its comprehensive, largely accurate characterization of economic mechanisms that survive in modern economics; and also for its effective use of rhetorical technique, including structuring the work to contrast real world examples of free and fettered markets.

a. Black Book of Communism
b. The Rise and Fall of the Great Powers
c. The Bell Curve
d. Wealth of Nations

Chapter 2. EFFICIENTY, EXCHANGE, AND COMPARATIVE ADVANTAGE

40. Manifesto of the Communist Party , often referred to as The _____, was first published on February 21, 1848, and is one of the world's most influential political manuscripts. Commissioned by the Communist League and written by communist theorists Karl Marx and Friedrich Engels, it laid out the League's purposes and program. It presents an analytical approach to the class struggle and the problems of capitalism, rather than a prediction of communism's potential future forms.
   a. Differential and Absolute Ground Rent
   b. Labour power
   c. Dialectical materialism
   d. Communist Manifesto

41.

_____ was a German philosopher, political economist, historian, political theorist, sociologist, communist and revolutionary credited as the founder of communism.

Marx summarized his approach to history and politics in the opening line of the first chapter of The Communist Manifesto : e;The history of all hitherto existing society is the history of class struggles.e; Marx argued that capitalism, like previous socioeconomic systems, will produce internal tensions which will lead to its destruction. Just as capitalism replaced feudalism, socialism will in its turn replace capitalism and lead to a stateless, classless society which will emerge after a transitional period, the 'dictatorship of the proletariat'.

   a. Neo-Gramscianism
   b. Adam Smith
   c. Marxism
   d. Karl Heinrich Marx

42. A _____ is an aspect of the tax code designed to incentivize a certain type of behavior. This may be accomplished through means including tax holidays or tax deductions.
   a. Nil-rate band
   b. Current use
   c. General nondiscrimination
   d. Tax incentive

Chapter 2. EFFICIENTY, EXCHANGE, AND COMPARATIVE ADVANTAGE 17

43. A _____ is:

- Rewrite _____, in generative grammar and computer science
- Standardization, a formal and widely-accepted statement, fact, definition, or qualification
- Operation, a determinate _____ for performing a mathematical operation and obtaining a certain result (Mathematics, Logic)
    - Unary operation
    - Binary operation
- _____ of inference, a function from sets of formulae to formulae (Mathematics, Logic)
- _____ of thumb, principle with broad application that is not intended to be strictly accurate or reliable for every situation. Also often simply referred to as a _____
- Moral, an atomic element of a moral code for guiding choices in human behavior
- Heuristic, a quantized '_____' which shows a tendency or probability for successful function
- A regulation, as in sports
- A Production _____, as in computer science
- Procedural law, a _____ set governing the application of laws to cases
    - A law, which may informally be called a '_____'
    - A court ruling, a decision by a court
- In the U.S. Government, a regulation mandated by Congress, but written or expanded upon by the Executive Branch.
- Norm (sociology), an informal but widely accepted _____, concept, truth, definition, or qualification (social norms, legal norms, coding norms)
- Norm (philosophy), a kind of sentence or a reason to act, feel or believe
- 'Rulership' is the concept of governance by a government:
    - Military _____, governance by a military body
    - Monastic _____, a collection of precepts that guides the life of monks or nuns in a religious order where the superior holds the place of Christ
- Slide _____

- '_____,' a song by Ayumi Hamasaki
- '_____,' a song by rapper Nas
- '_____s,' an album by the band The Whitest Boy Alive
- _____s: Pyaar Ka Superhit Formula, a 2003 Bollywood film
- ruler, an instrument for measuring lengths
- _____, a component of an astrolabe, circumferator or similar instrument
- The _____s, a bestselling self-help book
- _____ Project (Run Up-to-date Linux Everywhere), a project that aims to use up-to-date Linux software on old PCs
- _____ engine, a software system that helps managing business _____s
- Ja _____, a hip hop artist
    - R.U.L.E., a 2005 greatest hits album by rapper Ja _____
- '_____s,' a KMFDM song

a. Demand
c. Procter ' Gamble
b. Technocracy
d. Rule

Chapter 3. SUBSTITUTES EVERYWHERE: THE CONCEPT OF DEMAND

1. _____s (economically referred to as land or raw materials) occur naturally within environments that exist relatively undisturbed by mankind, in a natural form. A _____'s is often characterized by amounts of biodiversity existent in various ecosystems.

Mining, petroleum extraction, fishing, hunting, and forestry are generally considered natural-resource industries.

   a. 1921 recession
   b. Natural resource
   c. 100-year flood
   d. 130-30 fund

2. Economics:

   - _____,the desire to own something and the ability to pay for it
   - _____ curve,a graphic representation of a _____ schedule
   - _____ deposit, the money in checking accounts
   - _____ pull theory,the theory that inflation occurs when _____ for goods and services exceeds existing supplies
   - _____ schedule,a table that lists the quantity of a good a person will buy it each different price
   - _____ side economics,the school of economics at believes government spending and tax cuts open economy by raising _____

   a. Variability
   b. McKesson ' Robbins scandal
   c. Production
   d. Demand

3. _____ is a slogan popularized by Karl Marx in his 1875 Critique of the Gotha Program. The phrase summarizes the principles that, under a communist system, every person should contribute to society to the best of his ability and consume from society in proportion to his needs, regardless of how much he has contributed. In the Marxist view, such an arrangement will be made possible by the abundance of goods and services that a developed communist society will produce; the idea is that there will be enough to satisfy everyone's needs.

   a. Proletarianization
   b. Temporal single-system interpretation
   c. Reserve army of labour
   d. From each according to his ability, to each according to his need

4. The _____ consists of a number of economic theories which describe the nature of the firm, company including its existence, its behaviour, and its relationship with the market.

In simplified terms, the _____ aims to answer these questions:

   1. Existence - why do firms emerge, why are not all transactions in the economy mediated over the market?
   2. Boundaries - why the boundary between firms and the market is located exactly there? Which transactions are performed internally and which are negotiated on the market?
   3. Organization - why are firms structured in such specific way? What is the interplay of formal and informal relationships?

Despite looking simple, these questions are not answered by the established economic theory, which usually views firms as given, and treats them as black boxes without any internal structure.

Chapter 3. SUBSTITUTES EVERYWHERE: THE CONCEPT OF DEMAND

The First World War period saw a change of emphasis in economic theory away from industry-level analysis which mainly included analysing markets to analysis at the level of the firm, as it became increasingly clear that perfect competition was no longer an adequate model of how firms behaved. Economic theory till then had focussed on trying to understand markets alone and there had been little study on understanding why firms or organisations exist.

- a. Khazzoom-Brookes postulate
- b. Policy Ineffectiveness Proposition
- c. Technology gap
- d. Theory of the firm

5. A _____ is a situation that involves losing one quality or aspect of something in return for gaining another quality or aspect. It implies a decision to be made with full comprehension of both the upside and downside of a particular choice.

In economics the term is expressed as opportunity cost, referring the most preferred alternative given up.

- a. Whitemail
- b. Trade-off
- c. Friedman-Savage utility function
- d. Nonmarket

6. _____ is the a method of technical and economic research of the systems for purpose to optimize a parity between system's consumer functions or properties and expenses to achieve those functions or properties.

This methodology for continuous perfection of production, industrial technologies, organizational structures was developed by Juryj Sobolev in 1948 at the 'Perm telephone factory'

- 1948 Juryj Sobolev - the first success in application of a method analysis at the 'Perm telephone factory' .
- 1949 - the first application for the invention as result of use of the new method.

Today in economically developed countries practically each enterprise or the company use methodology of the kind of functional-cost analysis as a practice of the quality management, most full satisfying to principles of standards of series ISO 9000.

- Interest of consumer not in products itself, but the advantage which it will receive from its usage.
- The consumer aspires to reduce his expenses
- Functions needed by consumer can be executed in the various ways, and, hence, with various efficiency and expenses. Among possible alternatives of realization of functions exist such in which the parity of quality and the price is the optimal for the consumer.

The goal of _____ is achievement of the highest consumer satisfaction of production at simultaneous decrease in all kinds of industrial expenses Classical _____ has three English synonyms - Value Engineering, Value Management, Value Analysis.

- a. Function cost analysis
- b. Monopoly wage
- c. Willingness to pay
- d. Staple financing

Chapter 3. SUBSTITUTES EVERYWHERE: THE CONCEPT OF DEMAND

7. _____s is the social science that studies the production, distribution, and consumption of goods and services. The term _____s comes from the Ancient Greek oá¼°κονομῖα from oá¼¶κος (oikos, 'house') + vÏŒμος (nomos, 'custom' or 'law'), hence 'rules of the house(hold)'. Current _____ models developed out of the broader field of political economy in the late 19th century, owing to a desire to use an empirical approach more akin to the physical sciences.

a. Economic
b. Energy economics
c. Inflation
d. Opportunity cost

8. _____ is a term used in economic research and policy debates. As with freedom generally, there are various definitions, but no universally accepted concept of _____. One major approach to _____ comes from the libertarian tradition emphasizing free markets and private property, while another extends the welfare economics study of individual choice, with greater _____ coming from a 'larger' (in some technical sense) set of possible choices.

a. International sanctions
b. Economic liberalization
c. Investment policy
d. Economic Freedom

9. _____ is sometimes referred to as _____, actually it means Economic Monetary Union.

First ideas of an economic and monetary union in Europe were raised well before establishing the European Communities. For example, already in the League of Nations, Gustav Stresemann asked in 1929 for a European currency (Link) against the background of an increased economic division due to a number of new nation states in Europe after WWI.

a. European Monetary System
b. Euro Interbank Offered Rate
c. Exchange rate mechanism
d. European Monetary Union

10. An economic and _____ is a single market with a common currency. It is to be distinguished from a mere currency union , which does not involve a single market. This is the fifth stage of economic integration.

a. Commercial invoice
b. Monetary Union
c. Free trade zone
d. Customs union

11. _____ is an online peer-reviewed magazine published by the Agricultural ' Applied Economics Association (AAEA) for readers interested in the policy and management of agriculture, the food industry, natural resources, rural communities, and the environment. _____ is published quarterly and is available free online. It is currently one of three outreach products offered by AAEA, along with the more timely Policy Issues and the forthcoming Shared Materials section of the AAEA Web site.

a. 100-year flood
b. Choices
c. 130-30 fund
d. 1921 recession

12. In economics, the _____ can be defined as the graph depicting the relationship between the price of a certain commodity, and the amount of it that consumers are willing and able to purchase at that given price. It is a graphic representation of a demand schedule. The _____ for all consumers together follows from the _____ of every individual consumer: the individual demands at each price are added together.

a. Kuznets curve
b. Wage curve
c. Cost curve
d. Demand curve

Chapter 3. SUBSTITUTES EVERYWHERE: THE CONCEPT OF DEMAND 21

13. _____ is the use of marginal concepts within economics. (Marginal concepts are associated with a specific change in the quantity used of a good or of a service, as opposed to some notion of the over-all significance of that class of good or service, or of some total quantity thereof.) The central concept of _____ proper is that of marginal utility, but marginalists following the lead of Alfred Marshall were further heavily dependent upon the concept of marginal physical productivity in their explanation of cost; and the neoclassical tradition that emerged from British _____ generally abandoned the concept of utility and gave marginal rates of substitution a more fundamental rôle in analysis.

    a. Just price
    b. Classical economics
    c. Marginalism
    d. Tendency of the rate of profit to fall

14. _____ is a broad label that refers to any individuals or households that use goods and services generated within the economy. The concept of a _____ is used in different contexts, so that the usage and significance of the term may vary.

Typically when business people and economists talk of _____s they are talking about person as _____, an aggregated commodity item with little individuality other than that expressed in the buy/not-buy decision.

    a. 100-year flood
    b. Consumer
    c. 130-30 fund
    d. 1921 recession

15. A _____ is a measure of the average price of consumer goods and services purchased by households. A _____ measures a price change for a constant market basket of goods and services from one period to the next within the same area (city, region, or nation.) It is a price index determined by measuring the price of a standard group of goods meant to represent the typical market basket of a typical urban consumer.

    a. Lipstick index
    b. CPI
    c. Cost-of-living index
    d. Consumer Price Index

16. _____ in economics and business is the result of an exchange and from that trade we assign a numerical monetary value to a good, service or asset. If Alice trades Bob 4 apples for an orange, the _____ of an orange is 4 apples. Inversely, the _____ of an apple is 1/4 oranges.

    a. Price war
    b. Price book
    c. Premium pricing
    d. Price

17. A _____ is a normalized average (typically a weighted average) of prices for a given class of goods or services in a given region, during a given interval of time. It is a statistic designed to help to compare how these prices, taken as a whole, differ between time periods or geographical locations.

Price indices have several potential uses.

    a. Two-part tariff
    b. Product sabotage
    c. Price Index
    d. Transactional Net Margin Method

18. _____ is a common concept in economics, and gives rise to derived concepts such as consumer debt. Generally _____ is defined by opposition to production. But the precise definition can vary because different schools of economists define production quite differently.

a. Foreclosure data providers
b. Consumption
c. Federal Reserve Bank Notes
d. Cash or share options

19. In economics, the _____ is an economic law that states that consumers buy more of a good when its price decreases and less when its price increases.

There are certain goods which do not follow this law. These include Veblen and Giffen goods

a. Law of demand
b. Financial crisis
c. Market failure
d. Georgism

20. _____ is an economic model based on price, utility and quantity in a market. It predicts that in a competitive market, price will function to equalize the quantity demanded by consumers, and the quantity supplied by producers, resulting in an economic equilibrium of price and quantity. The model incorporates other factors changing equilibrium as a shift of demand and/or supply.

a. Deferred gratification
b. Supply and demand
c. Rational addiction
d. Joint demand

21. A _____ occurs when an entity spends more money than it takes in. The opposite of a _____ is a budget surplus. Debt is essentially an accumulated flow of deficits.

a. Lump-sum tax
b. Public Financial Management
c. Funding body
d. Budget deficit

22. A _____ is an object whose consumption increases the utility of the consumer, for which the quantity demanded exceeds the quantity supplied at zero price. _____s are usually modeled as having diminishing marginal utility. The first individual purchase has high utility; the second has less.

a. Good
b. Pie method
c. Merit good
d. Composite good

23. In consumer theory, an _____ is a good that decreases in demand when consumer income rises, unlike normal goods, for which the opposite is observed. It is a good that consumers demand increases when their income increases. Inferiority, in this sense, is an observable fact relating to affordability rather than a statement about the quality of the good.

a. Export-oriented
b. Information good
c. Independent goods
d. Inferior good

24. In economics, _____s are any goods for which demand increases when income increases and falls when income decreases but price remains constant, i.e. with a positive income elasticity of demand. The term does not necessarily refer to the quality of the good.

Depending on the indifference curves, the amount of a good bought can either increase, decrease, or stay the same when income increases.

a. Financial contagion
b. Normal good
c. Bord halfpenny
d. Normative economics

Chapter 3. SUBSTITUTES EVERYWHERE: THE CONCEPT OF DEMAND

25. A _____ or complement good in economics is a good which is consumed with another good; its cross elasticity of demand is negative. - It is two goods that are bought and used together. This means that, if goods A and B were complements, more of good A being bought would result in more of good B also being bought.
    a. Manufactured goods
    b. Final good
    c. Free good
    d. Complementary good

26. In economics, _____ is a rise in the general level of prices of goods and services in an economy over a period of time. When the general price level rises, each unit of currency buys fewer goods and services; consequently, _____ is also a decline in the real value of money--a loss of purchasing power in the medium of exchange which is also the monetary unit of account in the economy. A chief measure of general price-level _____ is the general _____ rate, which is the percentage change in a general price index (normally the Consumer Price Index) over time.
    a. Energy economics
    b. Opportunity cost
    c. Economic
    d. Inflation

27. The _____ was written by Adam Smith in 1759. It provided the ethical, philosophical, psychological and methodological underpinnings to Smith's later works, including The Wealth of Nations (1776), A Treatise on Public Opulence (1764) (first published in 1937), Essays on Philosophical Subjects (1795), and Lectures on Justice, Police, Revenue, and Arms (1763) (first published in 1896.)

Broadly speaking, Smith followed the views of his mentor, Francis Hutcheson of the University of Glasgow, who divided moral philosophy into four parts: Ethics and Virtue; Private rights and Natural liberty; Familial rights (called Economics); and State and Individual rights (called Politics.)

    a. Butterfly Economics
    b. Capital and Interest
    c. Theory of Moral Sentiments
    d. Limits to Growth

28. _____ is the price of a commodity such as a good or service in terms of another; ie, the ratio of two prices. A _____ may be expressed in terms of a ratio between any two prices or the ratio between the price of one particular good and a weighted average of all other goods available in the market. A _____ is an opportunity cost.
    a. Food cooperative
    b. Relative price
    c. False shortage
    d. False economy

29. In economics, _____ is the ratio of the percent change in one variable to the percent change in another variable. It is a tool for measuring the responsiveness of a function to changes in parameters in a relative way. Commonly analyzed are _____ of substitution, price and wealth.
    a. Elasticity of demand
    b. ACEA agreement
    c. Elasticity
    d. ACCRA Cost of Living Index

30. The _____ or gross domestic income (GDI), a basic measure of an economy's economic performance, is the market value of all final goods and services produced within the borders of a nation in a year. _____ can be defined in three ways, all of which are conceptually identical. First, it is equal to the total expenditures for all final goods and services produced within the country in a stipulated period of time (usually a 365-day year.)
    a. Countercyclical
    b. Market structure
    c. Monopolistic competition
    d. Gross domestic product

Chapter 3. SUBSTITUTES EVERYWHERE: THE CONCEPT OF DEMAND

31. _____ is a misspelled phrase from Latin 'pro capite' phrase meaning per head with pro meaning 'per' or 'for each' and capite meaning 'head.' Both words together equate to the phrase 'for each head.'

It is usually used in the field of statistics to indicate the average per person for any given concern, such as income, crime rate, etc.

It is also used in wills to indicate that each of the named beneficiaries should receive, by devise or bequest, equal shares of the estate. This is in contrast to a per stirpes division, in which each branch of the inheriting family inherits an equal share of the estate.

- a. Sargan test
- b. False positive rate
- c. Population statistics
- d. Per capita

32. _____ was a survey conducted by the U.S. Department of Justice to gauge the prevalence of alcohol and illegal drug use among prior arrestees. It was a reformulation of the prior Drug Use Forecasting (DUF) program, focused on five drugs in particular: cocaine, marijuana, methamphetamine, opiates, and PCP.

Participants were randomly selected from arrest records in major metropolitan areas; because no personally identifying information is taken from each record chosen, the resulting data can be correlated to arrest rates, but not to the total population of persons charged.

- a. AD-IA Model
- b. ACCRA Cost of Living Index
- c. Arrestee Drug Abuse Monitoring
- d. ACEA agreement

33. _____ was a Scottish moral philosopher and a pioneer of political economy. One of the key figures of the Scottish Enlightenment, Smith is the author of The Theory of Moral Sentiments and An Inquiry into the Nature and Causes of the Wealth of Nations. The latter, usually abbreviated as The Wealth of Nations, is considered his magnum opus and the first modern work of economics.

- a. Adolf Hitler
- b. Alan Greenspan
- c. Adam Smith
- d. Adolph Fischer

34. _____ is the controlled distribution of resources and scarce goods or services. _____ controls the size of the ration, one's allotted portion of the resources being distributed on a particular day or at a particular time.

In economics, it is often common to use the word '_____' to refer to one of the roles that prices play in markets, while _____ is called 'non-price _____.' Using prices to ration means that those with the most money (or other assets) and who want a product the most are first to receive it.

- a. Rationing
- b. 100-year flood
- c. 130-30 fund
- d. 1921 recession

Chapter 4. OPPORTUNITY COST AND THE SUPPLY OF GOODS

1. In economics, the _____ is the term used to refer to the environment in which bonds are bought and sold between a central bank ' its regulated banks. It is not a free market process.

- To intervene in the 'business cycle', a central bank may choose to go into the _____ and buy or sell government bonds, which is known as _____ operations to increase reserves.

   a. Open Market   b. Outside money
   c. ACCRA Cost of Living Index   d. Inside money

2. _____ or economic opportunity loss is the value of the next best alternative foregone as the result of making a decision. _____ analysis is an important part of a company's decision-making processes but is not treated as an actual cost in any financial statement. The next best thing that a person can engage in is referred to as the _____ of doing the best thing and ignoring the next best thing to be done.
   a. Economic ideology   b. Industrial organization
   c. Economic   d. Opportunity cost

3. _____ is a broad label that refers to any individuals or households that use goods and services generated within the economy. The concept of a _____ is used in different contexts, so that the usage and significance of the term may vary.

Typically when business people and economists talk of _____s they are talking about person as _____, an aggregated commodity item with little individuality other than that expressed in the buy/not-buy decision.

   a. 100-year flood   b. 130-30 fund
   c. 1921 recession   d. Consumer

4. A _____ is a measure of the average price of consumer goods and services purchased by households. A _____ measures a price change for a constant market basket of goods and services from one period to the next within the same area (city, region, or nation.) It is a price index determined by measuring the price of a standard group of goods meant to represent the typical market basket of a typical urban consumer.
   a. Cost-of-living index   b. Consumer Price Index
   c. CPI   d. Lipstick index

5. _____ in economics and business is the result of an exchange and from that trade we assign a numerical monetary value to a good, service or asset. If Alice trades Bob 4 apples for an orange, the _____ of an orange is 4 apples. Inversely, the _____ of an apple is 1/4 oranges.
   a. Premium pricing   b. Price book
   c. Price   d. Price war

6. A _____ is a normalized average (typically a weighted average) of prices for a given class of goods or services in a given region, during a given interval of time. It is a statistic designed to help to compare how these prices, taken as a whole, differ between time periods or geographical locations.

Price indices have several potential uses.

Chapter 4. OPPORTUNITY COST AND THE SUPPLY OF GOODS

a. Product sabotage
b. Two-part tariff
c. Transactional Net Margin Method
d. Price Index

7. _____ is a fee paid on borrowed assets. It is the price paid for the use of borrowed money, or, money earned by deposited funds. Assets that are sometimes lent with _____ include money, shares, consumer goods through hire purchase, major assets such as aircraft, and even entire factories in finance lease arrangements.
   a. Interest
   b. Asset protection
   c. Insolvency
   d. Internal debt

8. In economics and finance, _____ is the change in total cost that arises when the quantity produced changes by one unit. It is the cost of producing one more unit of a good. Mathematically, the _____ function is expressed as the first derivative of the total cost (TC) function with respect to quantity (Q.)
   a. Variable cost
   b. Khozraschyot
   c. Quality costs
   d. Marginal cost

9. Economics:

   - _____, the desire to own something and the ability to pay for it
   - _____ curve, a graphic representation of a _____ schedule
   - _____ deposit, the money in checking accounts
   - _____ pull theory, the theory that inflation occurs when _____ for goods and services exceeds existing supplies
   - _____ schedule, a table that lists the quantity of a good a person will buy it each different price
   - _____ side economics, the school of economics at believes government spending and tax cuts open economy by raising _____

   a. McKesson ' Robbins scandal
   b. Variability
   c. Production
   d. Demand

10. In economics, the _____ can be defined as the graph depicting the relationship between the price of a certain commodity, and the amount of it that consumers are willing and able to purchase at that given price. It is a graphic representation of a demand schedule. The _____ for all consumers together follows from the _____ of every individual consumer: the individual demands at each price are added together.
    a. Wage curve
    b. Cost curve
    c. Kuznets curve
    d. Demand curve

11. In microeconomics, _____ is quite simply the conversion of inputs into outputs. It is an economic process that uses resources to create a good or service that is suitable for exchange. This can include manufacturing, storing, shipping, and packaging.
    a. MET
    b. Solved
    c. Red Guards
    d. Production

12. _____ is the price of a commodity such as a good or service in terms of another; ie, the ratio of two prices. A _____ may be expressed in terms of a ratio between any two prices or the ratio between the price of one particular good and a weighted average of all other goods available in the market. A _____ is an opportunity cost.

Chapter 4. OPPORTUNITY COST AND THE SUPPLY OF GOODS

a. False economy
c. Food cooperative
b. Relative price
d. False shortage

13. In economics, _____ is equal to total cost divided by the number of goods produced (the output quantity, Q.) It is also equal to the sum of average variable costs (total variable costs divided by Q) plus average fixed costs (total fixed costs divided by Q.) _____s may be dependent on the time period considered (increasing production may be expensive or impossible in the short term, for example.)

a. Average fixed cost
c. Average variable cost
b. Explicit cost
d. Average cost

14. In economics, _____ is the ratio of the percent change in one variable to the percent change in another variable. It is a tool for measuring the responsiveness of a function to changes in parameters in a relative way. Commonly analyzed are _____ of substitution, price and wealth.

a. ACCRA Cost of Living Index
c. Elasticity of demand
b. ACEA agreement
d. Elasticity

Chapter 5. SUPPLY AND DEMAND: A PROCESS OF COOPERATION

1. _____ was a survey conducted by the U.S. Department of Justice to gauge the prevalence of alcohol and illegal drug use among prior arrestees. It was a reformulation of the prior Drug Use Forecasting (DUF) program, focused on five drugs in particular: cocaine, marijuana, methamphetamine, opiates, and PCP.

Participants were randomly selected from arrest records in major metropolitan areas; because no personally identifying information is taken from each record chosen, the resulting data can be correlated to arrest rates, but not to the total population of persons charged.

   a. ACCRA Cost of Living Index
   b. ACEA agreement
   c. AD-IA Model
   d. Arrestee Drug Abuse Monitoring

2. _____ was a Scottish moral philosopher and a pioneer of political economy. One of the key figures of the Scottish Enlightenment, Smith is the author of The Theory of Moral Sentiments and An Inquiry into the Nature and Causes of the Wealth of Nations. The latter, usually abbreviated as The Wealth of Nations, is considered his magnum opus and the first modern work of economics.

   a. Adolph Fischer
   b. Alan Greenspan
   c. Adolf Hitler
   d. Adam Smith

3. In economics, _____ refers to the ability of a person or a country to produce a particular good at a lower marginal cost and opportunity cost than another person or country. It is the ability to produce a product most efficiently given all the other products that could be produced. It can be contrasted with absolute advantage which refers to the ability of a person or a country to produce a particular good at a lower absolute cost than another.

   a. Hot money
   b. Gravity model of trade
   c. Triffin dilemma
   d. Comparative advantage

4. Economics:

   - _____,the desire to own something and the ability to pay for it
   - _____ curve,a graphic representation of a _____ schedule
   - _____ deposit, the money in checking accounts
   - _____ pull theory,the theory that inflation occurs when _____ for goods and services exceeds existing supplies
   - _____ schedule,a table that lists the quantity of a good a person will buy it each different price
   - _____ side economics,the school of economics at believes government spending and tax cuts open economy by raising _____

   a. Production
   b. Variability
   c. McKesson ' Robbins scandal
   d. Demand

5. In finance, the term _____ describes various legal measures taken to ensure that debtors, whether individuals, businesses honor their debts and make an honest effort to repay the money that they owe. Generally regarded as a subdivision of tax law, _____ is most often enforced through a combination of audits and legal restrictions. For example, a provision of the Federal Debt Collection Procedure Act states that a person or organization indebted to the United States, against whom a judgment lien has been filed, is ineligible to receive a government grant.

Chapter 5. SUPPLY AND DEMAND: A PROCESS OF COOPERATION

a. Hard money loan
b. Carryback loan
c. Microcredit
d. Debt compliance

6. In economics, the _____ is the idea that a nation is better off when it produces goods and services for which it has a comparative advantage.
   a. Keynesian economics
   b. Recession
   c. Monopolistic competition
   d. Law of comparative advantage

7. _____ is an economic model based on price, utility and quantity in a market. It predicts that in a competitive market, price will function to equalize the quantity demanded by consumers, and the quantity supplied by producers, resulting in an economic equilibrium of price and quantity. The model incorporates other factors changing equilibrium as a shift of demand and/or supply.
   a. Rational addiction
   b. Joint demand
   c. Supply and demand
   d. Deferred gratification

8. _____ is a broad label that refers to any individuals or households that use goods and services generated within the economy. The concept of a _____ is used in different contexts, so that the usage and significance of the term may vary.

Typically when business people and economists talk of _____s they are talking about person as _____, an aggregated commodity item with little individuality other than that expressed in the buy/not-buy decision.

   a. Consumer
   b. 1921 recession
   c. 130-30 fund
   d. 100-year flood

9. A _____ is a measure of the average price of consumer goods and services purchased by households. A _____ measures a price change for a constant market basket of goods and services from one period to the next within the same area (city, region, or nation.) It is a price index determined by measuring the price of a standard group of goods meant to represent the typical market basket of a typical urban consumer.
   a. Lipstick index
   b. Consumer Price Index
   c. Cost-of-living index
   d. CPI

10. _____ in economics and business is the result of an exchange and from that trade we assign a numerical monetary value to a good, service or asset. If Alice trades Bob 4 apples for an orange, the _____ of an orange is 4 apples. Inversely, the _____ of an apple is 1/4 oranges.
    a. Premium pricing
    b. Price book
    c. Price
    d. Price war

11. A _____ is a normalized average (typically a weighted average) of prices for a given class of goods or services in a given region, during a given interval of time. It is a statistic designed to help to compare how these prices, taken as a whole, differ between time periods or geographical locations.

Price indices have several potential uses.

Chapter 5. SUPPLY AND DEMAND: A PROCESS OF COOPERATION

    a. Price Index
    b. Transactional Net Margin Method
    c. Product sabotage
    d. Two-part tariff

12. _____ is a fee paid on borrowed assets. It is the price paid for the use of borrowed money, or, money earned by deposited funds. Assets that are sometimes lent with _____ include money, shares, consumer goods through hire purchase, major assets such as aircraft, and even entire factories in finance lease arrangements.

    a. Internal debt
    b. Asset protection
    c. Insolvency
    d. Interest

13. A _____ is any systematic process enabling many market players to bid and ask: helping bidders and sellers interact and make deals. It is not just the price mechanism but the entire system of regulation, qualification, credentials, reputations and clearing that surrounds that mechanism and makes it operate in a social context.

Because a _____ relies on the assumption that players are constantly involved and unequally enabled, a _____ is distinguished specifically from a voting system where candidates seek the support of voters on a less regular basis.

    a. Contestable market
    b. Price mechanism
    c. Market system
    d. Competitive equilibrium

14. A _____ is the exclusive authority to determine how a resource is used, whether that resource is owned by government or by individuals. All economic goods have a _____s attribute. This attribute has three broad components

1. The right to use the good
2. The right to earn income from the good
3. The right to transfer the good to others

The concept of _____s as used by economists and legal scholars are related but distinct. The distinction is largely seen in the economists' focus on the ability of an individual or collective to control the use of the good.

    a. Holder in due course
    b. Post-sale restraint
    c. High-reeve
    d. Property right

15. _____s is the social science that studies the production, distribution, and consumption of goods and services. The term _____s comes from the Ancient Greek oá¼°κονομῖα from oá¼¶κος (oikos, 'house') + vÍŒμος (nomos, 'custom' or 'law'), hence 'rules of the house(hold)'. Current _____ models developed out of the broader field of political economy in the late 19th century, owing to a desire to use an empirical approach more akin to the physical sciences.

    a. Economic
    b. Energy economics
    c. Opportunity cost
    d. Inflation

16. _____ is a term used in economic research and policy debates. As with freedom generally, there are various definitions, but no universally accepted concept of _____. One major approach to _____ comes from the libertarian tradition emphasizing free markets and private property, while another extends the welfare economics study of individual choice, with greater _____ coming from a 'larger' (in some technical sense) set of possible choices.

Chapter 5. SUPPLY AND DEMAND: A PROCESS OF COOPERATION

a. Economic Freedom
b. International sanctions
c. Investment policy
d. Economic liberalization

17. _____ is an American economist and was the Chairman of the Federal Reserve of the United States from 1987 to 2006. He currently works as a private advisor and providing consulting for firms through his company, Greenspan Associates LLC.

First appointed Federal Reserve chairman by President Ronald Reagan in August 1987, he was reappointed at successive four-year intervals until retiring on January 31, 2006 after the second-longest tenure in the position.

a. Adolph Fischer
b. Adolf Hitler
c. Adam Smith
d. Alan Greenspan

18. _____ is an economic concept with commonplace familiarity. It is the price that a good or service is offered at, or will fetch, in the marketplace. It is of interest mainly in the study of microeconomics.

a. Paper trading
b. Market price
c. Market anomaly
d. Noisy market hypothesis

19. In economics and related disciplines, a _____ is a cost incurred in making an economic exchange. For example, most people, when buying or selling a stock, must pay a commission to their broker; that commission is a _____ of doing the stock deal. Or consider buying a banana from a store; to purchase the banana, your costs will be not only the price of the banana itself, but also the energy and effort it requires to find out which of the various banana products you prefer, where to get them and at what price, the cost of traveling from your house to the store and back, the time waiting in line, and the effort of the paying itself; the costs above and beyond the cost of the banana are the _____s.

a. Cost of poor quality
b. Cost allocation
c. Sliding scale fees
d. Transaction cost

20. Economic interventionism or _____ is an action in a Market economy taken by a government, beyond the basic regulation of fraud and enforcement of contracts, in an effort to affect its own economy. Economic intervention can be aimed at a variety of political or economic objectives, such as promoting economic growth, increasing employment, raising wages, raising or reducing prices, promoting equality, managing the money supply and interest rates, increasing profits, or addressing market failures. The intervention may to direct, or indirect as in the case of indicative planning.

a. ACCRA Cost of Living Index
b. ACEA agreement
c. AD-IA Model
d. Economic planning

21. Bartering is a medium in which goods or services are directly exchanged for other goods and/or services, without the use of money. It can be bilateral or multilateral, and usually exists parallel to monetary systems in most developed countries, though to a very limited extent. _____ usually replaces money as the method of exchange in times of monetary crisis, when the currency is unstable and devalued by hyperinflation.

a. Meitheal
b. Barter
c. New Economics Foundation
d. Community-based economics

22. A _____ occurs when an entity spends more money than it takes in. The opposite of a _____ is a budget surplus. Debt is essentially an accumulated flow of deficits.

Chapter 5. SUPPLY AND DEMAND: A PROCESS OF COOPERATION

a. Public Financial Management
b. Budget deficit
c. Lump-sum tax
d. Funding body

23. In economics, the _____ can be defined as the graph depicting the relationship between the price of a certain commodity, and the amount of it that consumers are willing and able to purchase at that given price. It is a graphic representation of a demand schedule. The _____ for all consumers together follows from the _____ of every individual consumer: the individual demands at each price are added together.
    a. Kuznets curve
    b. Wage curve
    c. Cost curve
    d. Demand curve

24. A _____ is a theoretical term that economists use to describe a market which is free from government intervention (i.e. no regulation, no subsidization, no single monetary system and no governmental monopolies.) In a _____, property rights are voluntarily exchanged at a price arranged solely by the mutual consent of sellers and buyers. By definition, buyers and sellers do not coerce each other, in the sense that they obtain each other's property without the use of physical force, threat of physical force, or fraud, nor is the coerced by a third party (such as by government via transfer payments) and they engage in trade simply because they both consent and believe that it is a good enough choice.
    a. Delegation
    b. Leninism
    c. Third camp
    d. Free market

25. _____ or economic opportunity loss is the value of the next best alternative foregone as the result of making a decision. _____ analysis is an important part of a company's decision-making processes but is not treated as an actual cost in any financial statement. The next best thing that a person can engage in is referred to as the _____ of doing the best thing and ignoring the next best thing to be done.
    a. Economic
    b. Opportunity cost
    c. Economic ideology
    d. Industrial organization

26. _____ is an offer (often competitive) of setting a price one is willing to pay for something. A price offer is called a bid. The term may be used in context of auctions, stock exchange, card games, or real estate transactions.
    a. Bord halfpenny
    b. Central limit order book
    c. Normal good
    d. Bidding

27. _____ is the acquisition of goods and/or services at the best possible total cost of ownership, in the right quantity and quality, at the right time, in the right place and from the right source for the direct benefit or use of corporations or individuals, generally via a contract. Simple _____ may involve nothing more than repeat purchasing. Complex _____ could involve finding long term partners - or even 'co-destiny' suppliers that might fundamentally commit one organization to another.
    a. Sole proprietorship
    b. Pre-emerging markets
    c. Golden umbrella
    d. Procurement

28. The _____ is a group of three respected economists who advise the President of the United States on economic policy. It is a part of the Executive Office of the President of the United States, and provides much of the economic policy of the White House. The council prepares the annual Economic Report of the President.
    a. Federal Reserve Bank Notes
    b. Council of Economic Advisers
    c. Constrained Pareto optimality
    d. Hybrid renewable energy systems

Chapter 5. SUPPLY AND DEMAND: A PROCESS OF COOPERATION

29. A _____ refers to any type debt instrument, such as a loan, bond, mortgage that does not have a fixed rate of interest over the life of the instrument. Such debt typically uses an index or other base rate for establishing the interest rate for each relevant period. One of the most common rates to use as the basis for applying interest rates is the London Inter-bank Offered Rate, or LIBOR
    a. Floating interest rate
    b. Moneylender
    c. Money market
    d. Disposal tax effect

30. _____ describes a deliberate attempt to interfere with the free and fair operation of the market and create artificial, false or misleading appearances with respect to the price of a security, commodity or currency. _____ is prohibited under Section 9(a)(2) of the Securities Exchange Act of 1934, and in Australia under Section s 1041A of the Corporations Act 2001. The Act defines _____ as transactions which create an artificial price or maintain an artificial price for a tradable security.
    a. Managerial economics
    b. Legal monopoly
    c. Market manipulation
    d. Net domestic product

31. An _____ is the price a borrower pays for the use of money they do not own, for instance a small company might borrow from a bank to kick start their business, and the return a lender receives for deferring the use of funds, by lending it to the borrower. _____s are normally expressed as a percentage rate over the period of one year.

_____s targets are also a vital tool of monetary policy and are used to control variables like investment, inflation, and unemployment.

    a. Arrow-Debreu model
    b. Enterprise value
    c. ACCRA Cost of Living Index
    d. Interest rate

32. _____ is the controlled distribution of resources and scarce goods or services. _____ controls the size of the ration, one's allotted portion of the resources being distributed on a particular day or at a particular time.

In economics, it is often common to use the word '_____' to refer to one of the roles that prices play in markets, while _____ is called 'non-price _____.' Using prices to ration means that those with the most money (or other assets) and who want a product the most are first to receive it.

    a. 130-30 fund
    b. Rationing
    c. 100-year flood
    d. 1921 recession

33. Necessary _____s:

If x is a necessary _____ of y, then the presence of y necessarily implies the presence of x. The presence of x, however, does not imply that y will occur.

Sufficient _____s:

If x is a sufficient _____ of y, then the presence of x necessarily implies the presence of y.

Chapter 5. SUPPLY AND DEMAND: A PROCESS OF COOPERATION

a. Political philosophy
b. Philosophy of economics
c. Materialism
d. Cause

34. An _____ is the magnum opus of the Scottish economist Adam Smith. It is a clearly written account of economics at the dawn of the Industrial Revolution, as well as a rhetorical piece written for the generally educated individual of the 18th century - advocating a free market economy as more productive and more beneficial to society.

The work is credited as a watershed in history and economics due to its comprehensive, largely accurate characterization of economic mechanisms that survive in modern economics; and also for its effective use of rhetorical technique, including structuring the work to contrast real world examples of free and fettered markets.

a. AD-IA Model
b. ACEA agreement
c. ACCRA Cost of Living Index
d. Inquiry into the Nature and Causes of the Wealth of Nations

35. The _____ was written by Adam Smith in 1759. It provided the ethical, philosophical, psychological and methodological underpinnings to Smith's later works, including The Wealth of Nations (1776), A Treatise on Public Opulence (1764) (first published in 1937), Essays on Philosophical Subjects (1795), and Lectures on Justice, Police, Revenue, and Arms (1763) (first published in 1896.)

Broadly speaking, Smith followed the views of his mentor, Francis Hutcheson of the University of Glasgow, who divided moral philosophy into four parts: Ethics and Virtue; Private rights and Natural liberty; Familial rights (called Economics); and State and Individual rights (called Politics.)

a. Limits to Growth
b. Theory of Moral Sentiments
c. Butterfly Economics
d. Capital and Interest

36. An Inquiry into the Nature and Causes of the _____ is the magnum opus of the Scottish economist Adam Smith. It is a clearly written account of economics at the dawn of the Industrial Revolution, as well as a rhetorical piece written for the generally educated individual of the 18th century - advocating a free market economy as more productive and more beneficial to society.

The work is credited as a watershed in history and economics due to its comprehensive, largely accurate characterization of economic mechanisms that survive in modern economics; and also for its effective use of rhetorical technique, including structuring the work to contrast real world examples of free and fettered markets.

a. Black Book of Communism
b. The Bell Curve
c. The Rise and Fall of the Great Powers
d. Wealth of Nations

37. A _____ is the transfer of wealth from one party (such as a person or company) to another. A _____ is usually made in exchange for the provision of goods, services or both, or to fulfill a legal obligation.

The simplest and oldest form of _____ is barter, the exchange of one good or service for another.

Chapter 5. SUPPLY AND DEMAND: A PROCESS OF COOPERATION

a. Soft count
c. Social gravity
b. Going concern
d. Payment

38. An Inquiry into the Nature and Causes of _____ is the magnum opus of the Scottish economist Adam Smith. It is a clearly written account of economics at the dawn of the Industrial Revolution, as well as a rhetorical piece written for the generally educated individual of the 18th century - advocating a free market economy as more productive and more beneficial to society.

The work is credited as a watershed in history and economics due to its comprehensive, largely accurate characterization of economic mechanisms that survive in modern economics; and also for its effective use of rhetorical technique, including structuring the work to contrast real world examples of free and fettered markets.

a. The Wealth of Nations
c. Capital and Interest
b. The Rise and Fall of the Great Powers
d. Banks and Politics in America

39. In economics, _____ pertains to how large a premium a consumer will place on enjoyment nearer in time over more remote enjoyment.

There is no absolute distinction that separates 'high' and 'low' _____, only comparisons with others either individually or in aggregate. Someone with a high _____ is focused substantially on his well-being in the present and the immediate future relative to the average person, while someone with low _____ places more emphasis than average on their well-being in the further future.

a. Temporal discounting
c. 130-30 fund
b. Time preference
d. 100-year flood

40. An _____ or Å"conomic system is a system that involves the production, distribution and consumption of goods and services between the entities in a particular society. It is the method used by society to produce and distribute goods and services. The _____ is composed of people and institutions, including their relationships to productive resources, such as through the convention of property.

a. Indicative planning
c. Intention economy
b. Economic system
d. Information economy

41. In finance and economics _____ or nominal rate of interest refers to the rate of interest before adjustment for inflation (in contrast with the real interest rate); or, for interest rates 'as stated' without adjustment for the full effect of compounding (also referred to as the nominal annual rate.) An interest rate is called nominal if the frequency of compounding (e.g. a month) is not identical to the basic time unit (normally a year.)

The real interest rate includes compensation for the lender's lost value due to inflation, whereas the _____ excludes inflation.

a. Risk-free interest rate
c. London Interbank Offered Rate
b. Fixed interest
d. Nominal interest rate

42. The '_____' is approximately the nominal interest rate minus the inflation rate Since the inflation rate over the course of a loan is not known initially, volatility in inflation represents a risk to both the lender and the borrower.

In economics and finance, an individual who lends money for repayment at a later point in time expects to be compensated for the time value of money, or not having the use of that money while it is lent.

a. Reflation
b. Cost-push inflation
c. Real interest rate
d. Core inflation

43. A _____ is a variable associated with an increased risk of disease or infection. _____s are correlational and not necessarily causal, because correlation does not imply causation. For example, being young cannot be said to cause measles, but young people are more at risk as they are less likely to have developed immunity during a previous epidemic.

a. Risk factor
b. Standardized mortality ratio
c. 130-30 fund
d. 100-year flood

44. In economics, _____ is a rise in the general level of prices of goods and services in an economy over a period of time. When the general price level rises, each unit of currency buys fewer goods and services; consequently, _____ is also a decline in the real value of money--a loss of purchasing power in the medium of exchange which is also the monetary unit of account in the economy. A chief measure of general price-level _____ is the general _____ rate, which is the percentage change in a general price index (normally the Consumer Price Index) over time.

a. Energy economics
b. Opportunity cost
c. Economic
d. Inflation

Chapter 6. SUPPLY AND DEMAND: ISSUES AND APPLICATIONS

1. _____s is the social science that studies the production, distribution, and consumption of goods and services. The term _____s comes from the Ancient Greek οἰκονομία from οἶκος (oikos, 'house') + νόμος (nomos, 'custom' or 'law'), hence 'rules of the house(hold)'. Current _____ models developed out of the broader field of political economy in the late 19th century, owing to a desire to use an empirical approach more akin to the physical sciences.
   a. Economic
   b. Inflation
   c. Energy economics
   d. Opportunity cost

2. _____ is a term used in economic research and policy debates. As with freedom generally, there are various definitions, but no universally accepted concept of _____. One major approach to _____ comes from the libertarian tradition emphasizing free markets and private property, while another extends the welfare economics study of individual choice, with greater _____ coming from a 'larger' (in some technical sense) set of possible choices.
   a. Economic Freedom
   b. Investment policy
   c. International sanctions
   d. Economic liberalization

3. Economics:

   - _____, the desire to own something and the ability to pay for it
   - _____ curve, a graphic representation of a _____ schedule
   - _____ deposit, the money in checking accounts
   - _____ pull theory, the theory that inflation occurs when _____ for goods and services exceeds existing supplies
   - _____ schedule, a table that lists the quantity of a good a person will buy it each different price
   - _____ side economics, the school of economics at believes government spending and tax cuts open economy by raising _____

   a. Production
   b. Demand
   c. McKesson ' Robbins scandal
   d. Variability

4. _____ in economics and business is the result of an exchange and from that trade we assign a numerical monetary value to a good, service or asset. If Alice trades Bob 4 apples for an orange, the _____ of an orange is 4 apples. Inversely, the _____ of an apple is 1/4 oranges.
   a. Price book
   b. Price
   c. Premium pricing
   d. Price war

5. _____ is an economic model based on price, utility and quantity in a market. It predicts that in a competitive market, price will function to equalize the quantity demanded by consumers, and the quantity supplied by producers, resulting in an economic equilibrium of price and quantity. The model incorporates other factors changing equilibrium as a shift of demand and/or supply.
   a. Joint demand
   b. Deferred gratification
   c. Rational addiction
   d. Supply and demand

6. In statistics, _____ indicates the strength and direction of a linear relationship between two random variables. That is in contrast with the usage of the term in colloquial speech, which denotes any relationship, not necessarily linear. In general statistical usage, _____ or co-relation refers to the departure of two random variables from independence.

Chapter 6. SUPPLY AND DEMAND: ISSUES AND APPLICATIONS

  a. Correlation
  b. 1921 recession
  c. 100-year flood
  d. 130-30 fund

7. A _____ is a government imposed limit on how high a price can be charged on a product. For a _____ to be effective, it must differ from the free market price. In the graph at right, the supply and demand curves intersect to determine the free-market quantity and price.
  a. Product sabotage
  b. Pricing
  c. Price ceiling
  d. Fire sale

8. _____ is a broad label that refers to any individuals or households that use goods and services generated within the economy. The concept of a _____ is used in different contexts, so that the usage and significance of the term may vary.

Typically when business people and economists talk of _____s they are talking about person as _____, an aggregated commodity item with little individuality other than that expressed in the buy/not-buy decision.

  a. 130-30 fund
  b. 100-year flood
  c. 1921 recession
  d. Consumer

9. A _____ is a measure of the average price of consumer goods and services purchased by households. A _____ measures a price change for a constant market basket of goods and services from one period to the next within the same area (city, region, or nation.) It is a price index determined by measuring the price of a standard group of goods meant to represent the typical market basket of a typical urban consumer.
  a. Lipstick index
  b. Cost-of-living index
  c. CPI
  d. Consumer Price Index

10. A _____ is a normalized average (typically a weighted average) of prices for a given class of goods or services in a given region, during a given interval of time. It is a statistic designed to help to compare how these prices, taken as a whole, differ between time periods or geographical locations.

Price indices have several potential uses.

  a. Product sabotage
  b. Two-part tariff
  c. Transactional Net Margin Method
  d. Price Index

11. An _____ or Å"conomic system is a system that involves the production, distribution and consumption of goods and services between the entities in a particular society. It is the method used by society to produce and distribute goods and services. The _____ is composed of people and institutions, including their relationships to productive resources, such as through the convention of property.
  a. Information economy
  b. Intention economy
  c. Indicative planning
  d. Economic system

12. _____ is an economic concept with commonplace familiarity. It is the price that a good or service is offered at, or will fetch, in the marketplace. It is of interest mainly in the study of microeconomics.

Chapter 6. SUPPLY AND DEMAND: ISSUES AND APPLICATIONS

a. Market anomaly
b. Market price
c. Paper trading
d. Noisy market hypothesis

13. _____ is an agreement between business competitors to sell the same product or service at the same price. In general, it is an agreement intended to ultimately push the price of a product as high as possible, leading to profits for all the sellers. Price-fixing can also involve any agreement to fix, peg, discount or stabilize prices.
a. Cut-throat competition
b. Moral victory
c. Non-price competition
d. Price fixing

14. _____ is the controlled distribution of resources and scarce goods or services. _____ controls the size of the ration, one's allotted portion of the resources being distributed on a particular day or at a particular time.

In economics, it is often common to use the word '_____' to refer to one of the roles that prices play in markets, while _____ is called 'non-price _____.' Using prices to ration means that those with the most money (or other assets) and who want a product the most are first to receive it.

a. Rationing
b. 1921 recession
c. 100-year flood
d. 130-30 fund

15. _____, or a _____ is the concept of a resulting effect (cf. cause and effect, arising from another action. In general terms, it is used to indicate that all human actions, particularly crime and sin, have profound effects.
a. Variability
b. Consequence
c. Solved
d. Rule

16. The _____ is a group of three respected economists who advise the President of the United States on economic policy. It is a part of the Executive Office of the President of the United States, and provides much of the economic policy of the White House. The council prepares the annual Economic Report of the President.
a. Constrained Pareto optimality
b. Hybrid renewable energy systems
c. Federal Reserve Bank Notes
d. Council of Economic Advisers

17. In finance, the term _____ describes various legal measures taken to ensure that debtors, whether individuals, businesses honor their debts and make an honest effort to repay the money that they owe. Generally regarded as a subdivision of tax law, _____ is most often enforced through a combination of audits and legal restrictions. For example, a provision of the Federal Debt Collection Procedure Act states that a person or organization indebted to the United States, against whom a judgment lien has been filed, is ineligible to receive a government grant.
a. Microcredit
b. Hard money loan
c. Carryback loan
d. Debt compliance

18. In economics and sociology, an _____ is any factor (financial or non-financial) that enables or motivates a particular course of action, or counts as a reason for preferring one choice to the alternatives. It is an expectation that encourages people to behave in a certain way. Since human beings are purposeful creatures, the study of _____ structures is central to the study of all economic activity (both in terms of individual decision-making and in terms of co-operation and competition within a larger institutional structure.)
a. Isocost
b. Epstein-Zin preferences
c. Economic reform
d. Incentive

Chapter 6. SUPPLY AND DEMAND: ISSUES AND APPLICATIONS

19. In economics, _____ refers to the ability of a person or a country to produce a particular good at a lower marginal cost and opportunity cost than another person or country. It is the ability to produce a product most efficiently given all the other products that could be produced. It can be contrasted with absolute advantage which refers to the ability of a person or a country to produce a particular good at a lower absolute cost than another.
    a. Hot money
    b. Gravity model of trade
    c. Triffin dilemma
    d. Comparative advantage

20. _____ is a fee paid on borrowed assets. It is the price paid for the use of borrowed money, or, money earned by deposited funds. Assets that are sometimes lent with _____ include money, shares, consumer goods through hire purchase, major assets such as aircraft, and even entire factories in finance lease arrangements.
    a. Insolvency
    b. Internal debt
    c. Asset protection
    d. Interest

21. A _____ is a government- or group-imposed limit on how low a price can be charged for a product. In order for a _____ to be effective, it must be greater than the equilibrium price. An ineffective _____, below equilibrium price.

    A _____ can be set below the free-market equilibrium price.

    a. Flat rate
    b. Price markdown
    c. Two-part tariff
    d. Price floor

22. A _____ is the lowest hourly, daily or monthly wage that employers may legally pay to employees or workers. Equivalently, it is the lowest wage at which workers may sell their labor. Although _____ laws are in effect in a great many jurisdictions, there are differences of opinion about the benefits and drawbacks of a _____.
    a. Microfoundations
    b. Marginal propensity to consume
    c. Permanent war economy
    d. Minimum wage

23. In economics, a _____ may be either a subsidy or a price control, both with the intended effect of keeping the market price of a good higher than the competitive equilibrium level.

    In the case of a price control, a _____ is the minimum legal price a seller may charge, typically placed above equilibrium. It is the support of certain price levels at or above market values by the government.

    a. Payment schedule
    b. Labor intensity
    c. Marginal profit
    d. Price support

24. In economics, the _____ is the term used to refer to the environment in which bonds are bought and sold between a central bank ' its regulated banks. It is not a free market process.

    - To intervene in the 'business cycle', a central bank may choose to go into the _____ and buy or sell government bonds, which is known as _____ operations to increase reserves.

    a. ACCRA Cost of Living Index
    b. Inside money
    c. Outside money
    d. Open Market

Chapter 6. SUPPLY AND DEMAND: ISSUES AND APPLICATIONS

25. _____ or economic opportunity loss is the value of the next best alternative foregone as the result of making a decision. _____ analysis is an important part of a company's decision-making processes but is not treated as an actual cost in any financial statement. The next best thing that a person can engage in is referred to as the _____ of doing the best thing and ignoring the next best thing to be done.
   a. Economic ideology
   b. Industrial organization
   c. Economic
   d. Opportunity cost

26. A _____ is the transfer of wealth from one party (such as a person or company) to another. A _____ is usually made in exchange for the provision of goods, services or both, or to fulfill a legal obligation.

   The simplest and oldest form of _____ is barter, the exchange of one good or service for another.

   a. Going concern
   b. Payment
   c. Soft count
   d. Social gravity

27. To _____ is to impose a financial charge or other levy upon a taxpayer by a state or the functional equivalent of a state.

   _____es are also imposed by many subnational entities. _____es consist of direct _____ or indirect _____, and may be paid in money or as its labour equivalent (often but not always unpaid.)

   a. 100-year flood
   b. 1921 recession
   c. 130-30 fund
   d. Tax

28. In economics, the _____ can be defined as the graph depicting the relationship between the price of a certain commodity, and the amount of it that consumers are willing and able to purchase at that given price. It is a graphic representation of a demand schedule. The _____ for all consumers together follows from the _____ of every individual consumer: the individual demands at each price are added together.
   a. Kuznets curve
   b. Cost curve
   c. Wage curve
   d. Demand curve

29. A _____ is any systematic process enabling many market players to bid and ask: helping bidders and sellers interact and make deals. It is not just the price mechanism but the entire system of regulation, qualification, credentials, reputations and clearing that surrounds that mechanism and makes it operate in a social context.

   Because a _____ relies on the assumption that players are constantly involved and unequally enabled, a _____ is distinguished specifically from a voting system where candidates seek the support of voters on a less regular basis.

   a. Price mechanism
   b. Market system
   c. Contestable market
   d. Competitive equilibrium

30. A _____ is a consumption tax charged at the point of purchase for certain goods and services. The tax is usually set as a percentage by the government charging the tax. There is usually a list of exemptions.

Chapter 6. SUPPLY AND DEMAND: ISSUES AND APPLICATIONS

a. 100-year flood
b. Sales tax
c. 1921 recession
d. 130-30 fund

31. To tax is to impose a financial charge or other levy upon a taxpayer by a state or the functional equivalent of a state.

_____ are also imposed by many subnational entities. _____ consist of direct tax or indirect tax, and may be paid in money or as its labour equivalent (often but not always unpaid.)

a. 100-year flood
b. 1921 recession
c. 130-30 fund
d. Taxes

32. The _____ was written by Adam Smith in 1759. It provided the ethical, philosophical, psychological and methodological underpinnings to Smith's later works, including The Wealth of Nations (1776), A Treatise on Public Opulence (1764) (first published in 1937), Essays on Philosophical Subjects (1795), and Lectures on Justice, Police, Revenue, and Arms (1763) (first published in 1896.)

Broadly speaking, Smith followed the views of his mentor, Francis Hutcheson of the University of Glasgow, who divided moral philosophy into four parts: Ethics and Virtue; Private rights and Natural liberty; Familial rights (called Economics); and State and Individual rights (called Politics.)

a. Limits to Growth
b. Capital and Interest
c. Butterfly Economics
d. Theory of Moral Sentiments

33. In economics, _____ is the analysis of the effect of a particular tax on the distribution of economic welfare. _____ is said to 'fall' upon the group that, at the end of the day, bears the burden of the tax. The key concept is that the _____ or tax burden does not depend on where the revenue is collected, but on the price elasticity of demand and price elasticity of supply.

a. 100-year flood
b. 130-30 fund
c. 1921 recession
d. Tax incidence

34. The _____ was a worldwide economic downturn starting in most places in 1929 and ending at different times in the 1930s or early 1940s for different countries. It was the largest and most important economic depression in the 20th century, and is used in the 21st century as an example of how far the world's economy can fall. The _____ originated in the United States; historians most often use as a starting date the stock market crash on October 29, 1929, known as Black Tuesday.

a. British Empire Economic Conference
b. Wall Street Crash of 1929
c. Jarrow March
d. Great Depression

35. In economics and business decision-making, _____ are costs that cannot be recovered once they have been incurred. _____ are sometimes contrasted with variable costs, which are the costs that will change due to the proposed course of action, and prospective costs which are costs that will be incurred if an action is taken.

In traditional microeconomic theory, only variable costs are relevant to a decision.

Chapter 6. SUPPLY AND DEMAND: ISSUES AND APPLICATIONS

a. Halo effect
c. Hyperbolic discounting
b. Post-purchase rationalization
d. Sunk costs

36. The _____ was a regulatory body in the United States created by the Interstate Commerce Act of 1887, which was signed into law by President Grover Cleveland. The agency was abolished in 1995, and the agency's remaining functions were transferred to the Surface Transportation Board.

The Commission's five members were appointed by the President with the consent of the United States Senate.

a. Office of Thrift Supervision
c. Interstate Commerce Commission
b. ACEA agreement
d. ACCRA Cost of Living Index

37. In economics and finance, _____ is the change in total cost that arises when the quantity produced changes by one unit. It is the cost of producing one more unit of a good. Mathematically, the _____ function is expressed as the first derivative of the total cost (TC) function with respect to quantity (Q.)

a. Khozraschyot
c. Variable cost
b. Marginal cost
d. Quality costs

38. In economics, the _____ is the maximum amount a person would be willing to pay, sacrifice or exchange for a good.

Choice modelling techniques may be used to estimate the value of the _____ through a choice experiment.

a. Net pay
c. Global strategy
b. Round-tripping
d. Willingness to pay

39. A _____ is the exclusive authority to determine how a resource is used, whether that resource is owned by government or by individuals. All economic goods have a _____s attribute. This attribute has three broad components

1. The right to use the good
2. The right to earn income from the good
3. The right to transfer the good to others

The concept of _____s as used by economists and legal scholars are related but distinct. The distinction is largely seen in the economists' focus on the ability of an individual or collective to control the use of the good.

a. Holder in due course
c. Property right
b. High-reeve
d. Post-sale restraint

40. A _____ occurs when an entity spends more money than it takes in. The opposite of a _____ is a budget surplus. Debt is essentially an accumulated flow of deficits.

a. Public Financial Management
c. Budget deficit
b. Lump-sum tax
d. Funding body

Chapter 7. PROFIT AND LOSS

1. _____ is a broad label that refers to any individuals or households that use goods and services generated within the economy. The concept of a _____ is used in different contexts, so that the usage and significance of the term may vary.

Typically when business people and economists talk of _____s they are talking about person as _____, an aggregated commodity item with little individuality other than that expressed in the buy/not-buy decision.

- a. 100-year flood
- b. Consumer
- c. 1921 recession
- d. 130-30 fund

2. A _____ is a measure of the average price of consumer goods and services purchased by households. A _____ measures a price change for a constant market basket of goods and services from one period to the next within the same area (city, region, or nation.) It is a price index determined by measuring the price of a standard group of goods meant to represent the typical market basket of a typical urban consumer.

- a. Cost-of-living index
- b. Lipstick index
- c. CPI
- d. Consumer Price Index

3. _____ in economics and business is the result of an exchange and from that trade we assign a numerical monetary value to a good, service or asset. If Alice trades Bob 4 apples for an orange, the _____ of an orange is 4 apples. Inversely, the _____ of an apple is 1/4 oranges.

- a. Price war
- b. Price book
- c. Premium pricing
- d. Price

4. A _____ is a normalized average (typically a weighted average) of prices for a given class of goods or services in a given region, during a given interval of time. It is a statistic designed to help to compare how these prices, taken as a whole, differ between time periods or geographical locations.

Price indices have several potential uses.

- a. Product sabotage
- b. Transactional Net Margin Method
- c. Two-part tariff
- d. Price Index

5. _____ is a fee paid on borrowed assets. It is the price paid for the use of borrowed money , or, money earned by deposited funds . Assets that are sometimes lent with _____ include money, shares, consumer goods through hire purchase, major assets such as aircraft, and even entire factories in finance lease arrangements.

- a. Insolvency
- b. Internal debt
- c. Asset protection
- d. Interest

6. In business and finance accounting, _____ is equal to the gross profit minus overheads minus interest payable plus/minus one off items for a given time period (usually: accounting period.)

A common synonym for '_____' when discussing financial statements (which include a balance sheet and an income statement) is the bottom line. This term results from the traditional appearance of an income statement which shows all allocated revenues and expenses over a specified time period with the resulting summation on the bottom line of the report.

Chapter 7. PROFIT AND LOSS

a. Salvage value
b. Net income
c. Depreciation
d. Net profit

7. _____ is a company's financial statement that indicates how the revenue is transformed into the net income The purpose of the _____ is to show managers and investors whether the company made or lost money during the period being reported.

The important thing to remember about an _____ is that it represents a period of time.

a. AD-IA Model
b. ACEA agreement
c. ACCRA Cost of Living Index
d. Income statement

8. Economic _____ is defined as an excess distribution to any factor in a production process above that which is required to induce the factor into the process or any excess above that which is necessary to keep the factor in its current use..

Classical Factor _____ is primarily concerned with the fee paid for the use of fixed (e.g. natural) resources. The classical definition is expressed as any excess payment above that required to induce or provide for production.

a. 1921 recession
b. Rent
c. 130-30 fund
d. 100-year flood

9. Necessary _____s:

If x is a necessary _____ of y, then the presence of y necessarily implies the presence of x. The presence of x, however, does not imply that y will occur.

Sufficient _____s:

If x is a sufficient _____ of y, then the presence of x necessarily implies the presence of y.

a. Materialism
b. Political philosophy
c. Philosophy of economics
d. Cause

10. The _____ is a group of three respected economists who advise the President of the United States on economic policy. It is a part of the Executive Office of the President of the United States, and provides much of the economic policy of the White House. The council prepares the annual Economic Report of the President.

a. Constrained Pareto optimality
b. Hybrid renewable energy systems
c. Federal Reserve Bank Notes
d. Council of Economic Advisers

11. _____s is the social science that studies the production, distribution, and consumption of goods and services. The term _____s comes from the Ancient Greek oá¼°κονομῖα from oá¼¶κος (oikos, 'house') + vïŒµος (nomos, 'custom' or 'law'), hence 'rules of the house(hold)'. Current _____ models developed out of the broader field of political economy in the late 19th century, owing to a desire to use an empirical approach more akin to the physical sciences.

Chapter 7. PROFIT AND LOSS

a. Inflation
b. Energy economics
c. Opportunity cost
d. Economic

12. An _____ is the magnum opus of the Scottish economist Adam Smith. It is a clearly written account of economics at the dawn of the Industrial Revolution, as well as a rhetorical piece written for the generally educated individual of the 18th century - advocating a free market economy as more productive and more beneficial to society.

The work is credited as a watershed in history and economics due to its comprehensive, largely accurate characterization of economic mechanisms that survive in modern economics; and also for its effective use of rhetorical technique, including structuring the work to contrast real world examples of free and fettered markets.

a. ACCRA Cost of Living Index
b. ACEA agreement
c. AD-IA Model
d. Inquiry into the Nature and Causes of the Wealth of Nations

13. _____s (economically referred to as land or raw materials) occur naturally within environments that exist relatively undisturbed by mankind, in a natural form. A _____'s is often characterized by amounts of biodiversity existent in various ecosystems.

Mining, petroleum extraction, fishing, hunting, and forestry are generally considered natural-resource industries.

a. 100-year flood
b. 130-30 fund
c. 1921 recession
d. Natural resource

14. An Inquiry into the Nature and Causes of the _____ is the magnum opus of the Scottish economist Adam Smith. It is a clearly written account of economics at the dawn of the Industrial Revolution, as well as a rhetorical piece written for the generally educated individual of the 18th century - advocating a free market economy as more productive and more beneficial to society.

The work is credited as a watershed in history and economics due to its comprehensive, largely accurate characterization of economic mechanisms that survive in modern economics; and also for its effective use of rhetorical technique, including structuring the work to contrast real world examples of free and fettered markets.

a. Wealth of Nations
b. The Bell Curve
c. The Rise and Fall of the Great Powers
d. Black Book of Communism

15. A _____ refers to any type debt instrument, such as a loan, bond, mortgage that does not have a fixed rate of interest over the life of the instrument. Such debt typically uses an index or other base rate for establishing the interest rate for each relevant period. One of the most common rates to use as the basis for applying interest rates is the London Inter-bank Offered Rate, or LIBOR

a. Money market
b. Disposal tax effect
c. Floating interest rate
d. Moneylender

Chapter 7. PROFIT AND LOSS

16. An _____ or Ä"conomic system is a system that involves the production, distribution and consumption of goods and services between the entities in a particular society. It is the method used by society to produce and distribute goods and services. The _____ is composed of people and institutions, including their relationships to productive resources, such as through the convention of property.

   a. Indicative planning
   b. Intention economy
   c. Economic system
   d. Information economy

17. The accounting equation relates assets, _____, and owner's equity:

   Assets = _____ + Owner's Equity

The accounting equation is the mathematical structure of the balance sheet.

The Australian Accounting Research Foundation defines _____ as: 'future sacrifice of economic benefits that the entity is presently obliged to make to other entities as a result of past transactions and other past events.'

Probably the most accepted accounting definition of liability is the one used by the International Accounting Standards Board (IASB.) The following is a quotation from IFRS Framework:

A liability is a present obligation of the enterprise arising from past events, the settlement of which is expected to result in an outflow from the enterprise of resources embodying economic benefits

-

Regulations as to the recognition of _____ are different all over the world, but are roughly similar to those of the IASB.

   a. Liabilities
   b. Community property
   c. Coase theorem
   d. Competition law theory

18. A _____ is an economy based on the division of labor in which the prices of goods and services are determined in a free price system set by supply and demand. This is often contrasted with a planned economy, in which a central government determines the price of goods and services using a fixed price system. Market economies are contrasted with mixed economy where the price system is not entirely free but under some government control that is not extensive enough to constitute a planned economy.

   a. Network Economy
   b. Market economy
   c. Nutritional Economics
   d. Commons-based peer production

19. An Inquiry into the Nature and Causes of _____ is the magnum opus of the Scottish economist Adam Smith. It is a clearly written account of economics at the dawn of the Industrial Revolution, as well as a rhetorical piece written for the generally educated individual of the 18th century - advocating a free market economy as more productive and more beneficial to society.

The work is credited as a watershed in history and economics due to its comprehensive, largely accurate characterization of economic mechanisms that survive in modern economics; and also for its effective use of rhetorical technique, including structuring the work to contrast real world examples of free and fettered markets.

   a. The Rise and Fall of the Great Powers
   b. Capital and Interest
   c. The Wealth of Nations
   d. Banks and Politics in America

20. _____ is that which is owed; usually referencing assets owed, but the term can also cover moral obligations and other interactions not requiring money. In the case of assets, _____ is a means of using future purchasing power in the present before a summation has been earned. Some companies and corporations use _____ as a part of their overall corporate finance strategy.
   a. Debenture
   b. Hard money loan
   c. Collateral Management
   d. Debt

21. _____ is a term used in economic research and policy debates. As with freedom generally, there are various definitions, but no universally accepted concept of _____. One major approach to _____ comes from the libertarian tradition emphasizing free markets and private property, while another extends the welfare economics study of individual choice, with greater _____ coming from a 'larger' (in some technical sense) set of possible choices.
   a. Investment policy
   b. International sanctions
   c. Economic liberalization
   d. Economic Freedom

22. _____ is sometimes referred to as _____, actually it means Economic Monetary Union.

First ideas of an economic and monetary union in Europe were raised well before establishing the European Communities. For example, already in the League of Nations, Gustav Stresemann asked in 1929 for a European currency (Link) against the background of an increased economic division due to a number of new nation states in Europe after WWI.

   a. Euro Interbank Offered Rate
   b. European Monetary Union
   c. Exchange rate mechanism
   d. European Monetary System

23. An economic and _____ is a single market with a common currency. It is to be distinguished from a mere currency union, which does not involve a single market. This is the fifth stage of economic integration.
   a. Free trade zone
   b. Commercial invoice
   c. Customs union
   d. Monetary Union

24. _____ is the difference between price and the costs of bringing to market whatever it is that is accounted as an enterprise (whether by harvest, extraction, manufacture, or purchase) in terms of the component costs of delivered goods and/or services and any operating or other expenses.

A key difficulty in measuring profit is in defining costs. Pure economic monetary profits can be zero or negative even in competitive equilibrium when accounted monetized costs exceed monetized price.

Chapter 7. PROFIT AND LOSS

a. Operating profit
b. Accounting profit
c. ACCRA Cost of Living Index
d. Economic profit

25. In economics, _____ is the difference between a company's total revenue and its opportunity costs. It is the increase in wealth that an investor has from making an investment, taking into consideration all costs associated with that investment including the opportunity cost of capital.

Profit is the factor income of the entrepreneur.

a. ACCRA Cost of Living Index
b. Operating profit
c. Economic profit
d. Accounting profit

26. An _____ is an easy accounted cost, such as wage, rent and materials. It can be transacted in the form of money payment and is lost directly, as opposed to monetary implicit costs.

a. Average fixed cost
b. Inventory valuation
c. Average variable cost
d. Explicit cost

27. In economics, an _____ occurs when one foregoes an alternative action but does not make an actual payment. (For instance, the explicit cost of a night at the movies includes the moviegoer's ticket and soda, but the _____ includes the pay he would have earned if he had chosen to work instead.) _____ s are related to forgone benefits of any single transaction.

a. External sector
b. Implicit cost
c. Ostrich strategy
d. Overnight trade

28. In economics, the _____ is that part of the economy which is both run for private profit and is not controlled by the state. By contrast, enterprises that are part of the state are part of the public sector; private, non-profit organizations are regarded as part of the voluntary sector.

A variety of legal structures exist for _____ business organizations, depending on the jurisdiction in which they have their legal domicile.

a. Secondary sector of the economy
b. Primary products
c. Standard Industrial Classification
d. Private sector

29. In microeconomics, _____ is quite simply the conversion of inputs into outputs. It is an economic process that uses resources to create a good or service that is suitable for exchange. This can include manufacturing, storing, shipping, and packaging.

a. Production
b. Red Guards
c. MET
d. Solved

30. The _____ is the part of economic and administrative life that deals with the delivery of goods and services by and for the government, whether national, regional or local/municipal.

Examples of _____ activity range from delivering social security, administering urban planning and organising national defenses.

Chapter 7. PROFIT AND LOSS

The organization of the _____ can take several forms, including:

- Direct administration funded through taxation; the delivering organization generally has no specific requirement to meet commercial success criteria, and production decisions are determined by government.
- Publicly owned corporations (in some contexts, especially manufacturing, 'state-owned enterprises'); which differ from direct administration in that they have greater commercial freedoms and are expected to operate according to commercial criteria, and production decisions are not generally taken by government (although goals may be set for them by government.)
- Partial outsourcing (of the scale many businesses do, e.g. for IT services), is considered a _____ model.

A borderline form is

- Complete outsourcing or contracting out, with a privately owned corporation delivering the entire service on behalf of government. This may be considered a mixture of private sector operations with public ownership of assets, although in some forms the private sector's control and/or risk is so great that the service may no longer be considered part of the _____.

a. Public sector
c. 130-30 fund
b. 100-year flood
d. Policy cycle

31. _____ refers to a business or organization attempting to acquire goods or services to accomplish the goals of the enterprise. Though there are several organizations that attempt to set standards in the _____ process, processes can vary greatly between organizations. Typically the word '_____' is not used interchangeably with the word 'procurement', since procurement typically includes Expediting, Supplier Quality, and Traffic and Logistics (T'L) in addition to _____.
   a. Purchasing
   b. 130-30 fund
   c. Free port
   d. 100-year flood

32. _____ is the number of goods/services that can be purchased with a unit of currency. For example, if you had taken one dollar to a store in the 1950s, you would have been able to buy a greater number of items than you would today, indicating that you would have had a greater _____ in the 1950s. Currency can be either a commodity money, like gold or silver, or fiat currency like US dollars.
   a. Human Poverty Index
   b. Genuine progress indicator
   c. Compliance cost
   d. Purchasing power

33. Recovery at law for pure _____ is restricted under some circumstances in some jurisdictions, in particular in tort in common law jurisdictions, for fear that it is potentially unlimited and could represent a 'crushing liability' against which parties would find it impossible to insure. U.S. Judge Benjamin N. Cardozo described it as, 'liability in an indeterminate amount, for an indeterminate time, to an indeterminate class'.

Chapter 7. PROFIT AND LOSS

Examples of pure _____ include:

- Loss of income suffered by a family whose principal earner dies in an accident. The physical injury is caused to the deceased, not the family.
- Loss of market value of a property owing to the inadequate specifications of foundations by an architect.
- Loss of production suffered by an enterprise whose electricity supply is interrupted by a contractor excavating a public utility.

The latter case is exemplified by the English case of Spartan Steel and Alloys Ltd v. Martin ' Co. Ltd Similar losses are also restricted in German law though not in French law.

a. ACCRA Cost of Living Index
c. ACEA agreement
b. Economic loss
d. AD-IA Model

34. An _____ is a person who has possession of an enterprise and assumes significant accountability for the inherent risks and the outcome. It is an ambitious leader who combines land, labor, and capital to create and market new goods or services. The term is a loanword from French and was first defined by the Irish economist Richard Cantillon.
    a. ACEA agreement
    b. Entrepreneur
    c. Expansionary policies
    d. ACCRA Cost of Living Index

35. _____ was a survey conducted by the U.S. Department of Justice to gauge the prevalence of alcohol and illegal drug use among prior arrestees. It was a reformulation of the prior Drug Use Forecasting (DUF) program, focused on five drugs in particular: cocaine, marijuana, methamphetamine, opiates, and PCP.

Participants were randomly selected from arrest records in major metropolitan areas; because no personally identifying information is taken from each record chosen, the resulting data can be correlated to arrest rates, but not to the total population of persons charged.

a. ACCRA Cost of Living Index
c. Arrestee Drug Abuse Monitoring
b. AD-IA Model
d. ACEA agreement

36. _____ is an economic system in which wealth, and the means of producing wealth, are privately owned. Through _____, the land, labor, and capital are owned, operated, and traded for the purpose of generating profits, without force or fraud, by private individuals either singly or jointly, and investments, distribution, income, production, pricing and supply of goods, commodities and services are determined by voluntary private decision in a market economy. A distinguishing feature of _____ is that each person owns his or her own labor and therefore is allowed to sell the use of it to employers.
    a. Late capitalism
    b. Socialism for the rich and capitalism for the poor
    c. Creative capitalism
    d. Capitalism

37. _____ was a Scottish moral philosopher and a pioneer of political economy. One of the key figures of the Scottish Enlightenment, Smith is the author of The Theory of Moral Sentiments and An Inquiry into the Nature and Causes of the Wealth of Nations. The latter, usually abbreviated as The Wealth of Nations, is considered his magnum opus and the first modern work of economics.

Chapter 7. PROFIT AND LOSS

a. Alan Greenspan
b. Adolph Fischer
c. Adam Smith
d. Adolf Hitler

38. In economics, the _____ is the agent who receives the net income (income after deducting all costs.) Residual claimancy is generally required in order for there to be Moral Hazard, which is a problem typical of information asymmetry. This is specifically the case for the Principal-agent problem.

a. Frontier markets
b. Free contract
c. Horizontal merger
d. Residual claimant

39. In economics and finance, _____ is the change in total cost that arises when the quantity produced changes by one unit. It is the cost of producing one more unit of a good. Mathematically, the _____ function is expressed as the first derivative of the total cost (TC) function with respect to quantity (Q.)

a. Marginal cost
b. Khozraschyot
c. Variable cost
d. Quality costs

40. In microeconomics, _____ is the extra revenue that an additional unit of product will bring. It is the additional income from selling one more unit of a good; sometimes equal to price. It can also be described as the change in total revenue/change in number of units sold.

a. Long term
b. Marginal revenue
c. Market demand schedule
d. Reservation price

41. In economics and finance, _____ is the practice of taking advantage of a price differential between two or more markets: striking a combination of matching deals that capitalize upon the imbalance, the profit being the difference between the market prices. When used by academics, an _____ is a transaction that involves no negative cash flow at any probabilistic or temporal state and a positive cash flow in at least one state; in simple terms, a risk-free profit. A person who engages in _____ is called an arbitrageur--such as a bank or brokerage firm.

a. Alternext
b. Options Price Reporting Authority
c. Arbitrage
d. Electronic trading

42. _____ according to Onuoha (2007) is the practice of starting new organizations or revitalizing mature organizations, particularly new businesses generally in response to identified opportunities. _____ is often a difficult undertaking, as a vast majority of new businesses fail. Entrepreneurial activities are substantially different depending on the type of organization that is being started.

a. ACEA agreement
b. Entrepreneurship
c. Intrapreneurship
d. ACCRA Cost of Living Index

43. The _____ was an early English joint-stock company that was formed initially for pursuing trade with the East Indies, but that ended up trading with the Indian subcontinent and China. The oldest among several similarly formed European East India Companies, the Company was granted an English Royal Charter, under the name Governor and Company of Merchants of London Trading into the East Indies, by Elizabeth I on 31 December 1600. After a rival English company challenged its monopoly in the late 17th century, the two companies were merged in 1708 to form the United Company of Merchants of England Trading to the East Indies, commonly styled the Honourable _____, and abbreviated, HEast India Company; the Company was colloquially referred to as John Company, and in India as Company Bahadur .

Chapter 7. PROFIT AND LOSS

a. ACEA agreement
b. AD-IA Model
c. ACCRA Cost of Living Index
d. East India Company

44. In economics, the _____ is a historical inverse relation between the rate of unemployment and the rate of inflation in an economy. Stated simply, the lower the unemployment in an economy, the higher the rate of increase in nominal wages in the economy. Rate of Change of Wages against Unemployment, United Kingdom 1913-1948 from Phillips (1958)

William Phillips, a New Zealand born economist, wrote a paper in 1958 titled The Relationship between Unemployment and the Rate of Change of Money Wages in the United Kingdom 1861-1957, which was published in the quarterly journal Economica.

a. Lorenz curve
b. Phillips curve
c. Cost curve
d. Demand curve

45. _____ is an economic concept with commonplace familiarity. It is the price that a good or service is offered at, or will fetch, in the marketplace. It is of interest mainly in the study of microeconomics.

a. Market anomaly
b. Paper trading
c. Market price
d. Noisy market hypothesis

46. An _____ is a manufacturing process in which parts (usually interchangeable parts) are added to a product in a sequential manner using optimally planned logistics to create a finished product much faster than with handcrafting-type methods. The _____ developed by Ford Motor Company between 1908 and 1915 made _____s famous in the following decade through the social ramifications of mass production, such as the affordability of the Ford Model T and the introduction of high wages for Ford workers. However, the various preconditions for the development at Ford stretched far back into the 19th century, from the gradual realization of the dream of interchangeability, to the concept of reinventing workflow and job descriptions using analytical methods.

a. Assembly line
b. ACCRA Cost of Living Index
c. AD-IA Model
d. ACEA agreement

47. In economics, _____ refers to the ability of a person or a country to produce a particular good at a lower marginal cost and opportunity cost than another person or country. It is the ability to produce a product most efficiently given all the other products that could be produced. It can be contrasted with absolute advantage which refers to the ability of a person or a country to produce a particular good at a lower absolute cost than another.

a. Hot money
b. Gravity model of trade
c. Triffin dilemma
d. Comparative advantage

48. A _____ is something for which there is demand, but which is supplied without qualitative differentiation across a market. It is a product that is the same no matter who produces it, such as petroleum, notebook paper, or milk. In other words, copper is copper.

a. Commodity
b. Hard commodity
c. Soft commodity
d. 100-year flood

Chapter 7. PROFIT AND LOSS

49. In finance, _____ is a financial action that does not promise safety of the initial investment along with the return on the principal sum. _____ typically involves the lending of money or the purchase of assets, equity or debt but in a manner that has not been given thorough analysis or is deemed to have low margin of safety or a significant risk of the loss of the principal investment. The term, '_____,' which is formally defined as above in Graham and Dodd's 1934 text, Security Analysis, contrasts with the term 'investment,' which is a financial operation that, upon thorough analysis, promises safety of principal and a satisfactory return.

   a. Global Financial Centres Index
   b. Hybrid market
   c. Municipal Bond Arbitrage
   d. Speculation

50. _____, or a _____ is the concept of a resulting effect (cf. cause and effect, arising from another action. In general terms, it is used to indicate that all human actions, particularly crime and sin, have profound effects.

   a. Rule
   b. Variability
   c. Solved
   d. Consequence

51. The _____ is the world's largest physical commodity futures exchange, located in New York City. Its two principal divisions are the _____ and Commodity Exchange, Inc (COMEX) which were once separate but are now merged. The parent company of the _____, Inc., New York Mercantile ExchangeX Holdings, Inc.

   a. Commodity Exchange
   b. 100-year flood
   c. 130-30 fund
   d. New York Mercantile Exchange

52. Economics:

- _____,the desire to own something and the ability to pay for it
- _____ curve,a graphic representation of a _____ schedule
- _____ deposit, the money in checking accounts
- _____ pull theory,the theory that inflation occurs when _____ for goods and services exceeds existing supplies
- _____ schedule,a table that lists the quantity of a good a person will buy it each different price
- _____ side economics,the school of economics at believes government spending and tax cuts open economy by raising _____

   a. Production
   b. Demand
   c. McKesson ' Robbins scandal
   d. Variability

Chapter 7. PROFIT AND LOSS

53. A _____ is:

- Rewrite _____, in generative grammar and computer science
- Standardization, a formal and widely-accepted statement, fact, definition, or qualification
- Operation, a determinate _____ for performing a mathematical operation and obtaining a certain result (Mathematics, Logic)
    - Unary operation
    - Binary operation
- _____ of inference, a function from sets of formulae to formulae (Mathematics, Logic)
- _____ of thumb, principle with broad application that is not intended to be strictly accurate or reliable for every situation. Also often simply referred to as a _____
- Moral, an atomic element of a moral code for guiding choices in human behavior
- Heuristic, a quantized '_____' which shows a tendency or probability for successful function
- A regulation, as in sports
- A Production _____, as in computer science
- Procedural law, a _____ set governing the application of laws to cases
    - A law, which may informally be called a '_____'
    - A court ruling, a decision by a court
- In the U.S. Government, a regulation mandated by Congress, but written or expanded upon by the Executive Branch.
- Norm (sociology), an informal but widely accepted _____, concept, truth, definition, or qualification (social norms, legal norms, coding norms)
- Norm (philosophy), a kind of sentence or a reason to act, feel or believe
- 'Rulership' is the concept of governance by a government:
    - Military _____, governance by a military body
    - Monastic _____, a collection of precepts that guides the life of monks or nuns in a religious order where the superior holds the place of Christ
- Slide _____

- '_____,' a song by Ayumi Hamasaki
- '_____,' a song by rapper Nas
- '_____s,' an album by the band The Whitest Boy Alive
- _____s: Pyaar Ka Superhit Formula, a 2003 Bollywood film
- ruler, an instrument for measuring lengths
- _____, a component of an astrolabe, circumferator or similar instrument
- The _____s, a bestselling self-help book
- _____ Project (Run Up-to-date Linux Everywhere), a project that aims to use up-to-date Linux software on old PCs
- _____ engine, a software system that helps managing business _____s
- Ja _____, a hip hop artist
    - R.U.L.E., a 2005 greatest hits album by rapper Ja _____
- '_____s,' a KMFDM song

a. Technocracy
b. Demand
c. Procter ' Gamble
d. Rule

Chapter 7. PROFIT AND LOSS

54. A _____ is a set of exclusive rights granted by a state to an inventor or his assignee for a limited period of time in exchange for a disclosure of an invention.

The procedure for granting _____s, the requirements placed on the _____ee and the extent of the exclusive rights vary widely between countries according to national laws and international agreements. Typically, however, a _____ application must include one or more claims defining the invention which must be new, inventive, and useful or industrially applicable.

    a. Bona fide occupational qualification
    c. Bank regulation
    b. Long service leave
    d. Patent

55.

The _____ is an independent agency of the United States government, created, directed, and empowered by Congressional statute , and with the majority of its commissioners appointed by the current President. The _____ works towards six strategic goals in the areas of broadband, competition, the spectrum, the media, public safety and homeland security, and modernizing the _____.

    a. 100-year flood
    c. 1921 recession
    b. 130-30 fund
    d. Federal Communications Commission

56. _____ is the United States of America's federal assistance program, formerly known as 'welfare'. It began on July 1, 1997, and succeeded the Aid to Families with Dependent Children program, providing cash assistance to indigent American families with dependent children through the United States Department of Health and Human Services. Prior to 1997, the federal government designed the overall program requirements and guidelines, while states administered the program and determined eligibility for benefits.

    a. 1921 recession
    c. 130-30 fund
    b. 100-year flood
    d. Temporary Assistance for Needy Families

57. In economics, a _____ may be either a subsidy or a price control, both with the intended effect of keeping the market price of a good higher than the competitive equilibrium level.

In the case of a price control, a _____ is the minimum legal price a seller may charge, typically placed above equilibrium. It is the support of certain price levels at or above market values by the government.

    a. Payment schedule
    c. Marginal profit
    b. Labor intensity
    d. Price support

58. A _____ is the exclusive authority to determine how a resource is used, whether that resource is owned by government or by individuals. All economic goods have a _____s attribute. This attribute has three broad components

1. The right to use the good
2. The right to earn income from the good
3. The right to transfer the good to others

The concept of _____s as used by economists and legal scholars are related but distinct. The distinction is largely seen in the economists' focus on the ability of an individual or collective to control the use of the good.

a. Holder in due course
b. High-reeve
c. Post-sale restraint
d. Property right

59. A _____ is one who resides on and farms land owned by a landlord. Tenant farming is an agricultural production system in which landowners contribute their land and often a measure of operating capital and management; while _____s contribute their labour along with at times varying amounts of capital and management. Depending on the contract, tenants can make payments to the owner either of a fixed portion of the product, in cash or in a combination.

a. Rural tenancy
b. Teikei
c. Tenant farmer
d. Landwirtschaftliche Produktionsgenossenschaft

60. _____ is a financial mechanism in which a debtor obtains the right to delay payments to a creditor, for a defined period of time, in exchange for a charge or fee. Essentially, the party that owes money in the present purchases the right to delay the payment until some future date. The discount, or charge, is simply the difference between the original amount owed in the present and the amount that has to be paid in the future to settle the debt.

a. Maximum life span
b. Certified Risk Manager
c. Generalized linear model
d. Discounting

61. In finance, the term _____ describes various legal measures taken to ensure that debtors, whether individuals, businesses honor their debts and make an honest effort to repay the money that they owe. Generally regarded as a subdivision of tax law, _____ is most often enforced through a combination of audits and legal restrictions. For example, a provision of the Federal Debt Collection Procedure Act states that a person or organization indebted to the United States, against whom a judgment lien has been filed, is ineligible to receive a government grant.

a. Carryback loan
b. Microcredit
c. Hard money loan
d. Debt compliance

62. _____ is the value on a given date of a future payment or series of future payments, discounted to reflect the time value of money and other factors such as investment risk. _____ calculations are widely used in business and economics to provide a means to compare cash flows at different times on a meaningful 'like to like' basis.

Money value fluctuates over time: $100 today are not worth $100 in five years.

a. Tax shield
b. Present value of costs
c. Future value
d. Present value

63. _____ is the a method of technical and economic research of the systems for purpose to optimize a parity between system's consumer functions or properties and expenses to achieve those functions or properties.

Chapter 7. PROFIT AND LOSS

This methodology for continuous perfection of production, industrial technologies, organizational structures was developed by Juryj Sobolev in 1948 at the 'Perm telephone factory'

- 1948 Juryj Sobolev - the first success in application of a method analysis at the 'Perm telephone factory' .
- 1949 - the first application for the invention as result of use of the new method.

Today in economically developed countries practically each enterprise or the company use methodology of the kind of functional-cost analysis as a practice of the quality management, most full satisfying to principles of standards of series ISO 9000.

- Interest of consumer not in products itself, but the advantage which it will receive from its usage.
- The consumer aspires to reduce his expenses
- Functions needed by consumer can be executed in the various ways, and, hence, with various efficiency and expenses. Among possible alternatives of realization of functions exist such in which the parity of quality and the price is the optimal for the consumer.

The goal of _____ is achievement of the highest consumer satisfaction of production at simultaneous decrease in all kinds of industrial expenses Classical _____ has three English synonyms - Value Engineering, Value Management, Value Analysis.

a. Monopoly wage
c. Staple financing
b. Willingness to pay
d. Function cost analysis

64. The _____ was a worldwide economic downturn starting in most places in 1929 and ending at different times in the 1930s or early 1940s for different countries. It was the largest and most important economic depression in the 20th century, and is used in the 21st century as an example of how far the world's economy can fall. The _____ originated in the United States; historians most often use as a starting date the stock market crash on October 29, 1929, known as Black Tuesday.

a. British Empire Economic Conference
c. Jarrow March
b. Wall Street Crash of 1929
d. Great Depression

65. Discounting is a financial mechanism in which a debtor obtains the right to delay payments to a creditor, for a defined period of time, in exchange for a charge or fee. Essentially, the party that owes money in the present purchases the right to delay the payment until some future date. The _____, or charge, is simply the difference between the original amount owed in the present and the amount that has to be paid in the future to settle the debt.

a. Discount
c. Certified Risk Manager
b. Reinsurance
d. Reliability theory

66. The _____ is an interest rate a central bank charges depository institutions that borrow reserves from it.

Chapter 7. PROFIT AND LOSS

The term _____ has two meanings:

- the same as interest rate; the term 'discount' does not refer to the meaning of the word, but to the purpose of using the quantity, such as computations of present value, e.g. net present value or discounted cash flow

- the annual effective _____, which is the annual interest divided by the capital including that interest; this rate is lower than the interest rate; it corresponds to using the value after a year as the nominal value, and seeing the initial value as the nominal value minus a discount; it is used for Treasury Bills and similar financial instruments

The annual effective _____ is the annual interest divided by the capital including that interest, which is the interest rate divided by 100% plus the interest rate. It is the annual discount factor to be applied to the future cash flow, to find the discount, subtracted from a future value to find the value one year earlier.

For example, suppose there is a government bond that sells for $95 and pays $100 in a year's time.

- a. Stochastic volatility
- b. Discount rate
- c. Perpetuity
- d. Johansen test

67. In economics, _____ is a rise in the general level of prices of goods and services in an economy over a period of time. When the general price level rises, each unit of currency buys fewer goods and services; consequently, _____ is also a decline in the real value of money--a loss of purchasing power in the medium of exchange which is also the monetary unit of account in the economy. A chief measure of general price-level _____ is the general _____ rate, which is the percentage change in a general price index (normally the Consumer Price Index) over time.
- a. Inflation
- b. Opportunity cost
- c. Energy economics
- d. Economic

68. A _____ is a variable associated with an increased risk of disease or infection. _____s are correlational and not necessarily causal, because correlation does not imply causation. For example, being young cannot be said to cause measles, but young people are more at risk as they are less likely to have developed immunity during a previous epidemic.
- a. Standardized mortality ratio
- b. Risk factor
- c. 130-30 fund
- d. 100-year flood

Chapter 8. COMPETITION AND MONOPOLY

1. _____ has several particular meanings:

   - in mathematics
     - _____ function
     - Euler _____
     - _____
     - _____ subgroup
     - method of _____s (partial differential equations)
   - in physics and engineering
     - any _____ curve that shows the relationship between certain input- and output parameters, e.g.
     - an I-V or current-voltage _____ is the current in a circuit as a function of the applied voltage
     - Receiver-Operator _____
   - in fiction
     - in Dungeons ' Dragons, _____ is another name for ability score

   a. Russian financial crisis
   b. Demand
   c. Characteristic
   d. Technocracy

2. In economics, a _____ exists when a specific individual or enterprise has sufficient control over a particular product or service to determine significantly the terms on which other individuals shall have access to it. Monopolies are thus characterized by a lack of economic competition for the good or service that they provide and a lack of viable substitute goods. The verb 'monopolize' refers to the process by which a firm gains persistently greater market share than what is expected under perfect competition.

   a. 130-30 fund
   b. Monopoly
   c. 1921 recession
   d. 100-year flood

3. _____s is the social science that studies the production, distribution, and consumption of goods and services. The term _____s comes from the Ancient Greek oá¼°κονομῖα from oá¼¶κος (oikos, 'house') + vῐŒμος (nomos, 'custom' or 'law'), hence 'rules of the house(hold)'. Current _____ models developed out of the broader field of political economy in the late 19th century, owing to a desire to use an empirical approach more akin to the physical sciences.

   a. Energy economics
   b. Economic
   c. Inflation
   d. Opportunity cost

4. _____ is a term used in economic research and policy debates. As with freedom generally, there are various definitions, but no universally accepted concept of _____. One major approach to _____ comes from the libertarian tradition emphasizing free markets and private property, while another extends the welfare economics study of individual choice, with greater _____ coming from a 'larger' (in some technical sense) set of possible choices.

   a. International sanctions
   b. Economic Freedom
   c. Investment policy
   d. Economic liberalization

Chapter 8. COMPETITION AND MONOPOLY

5. Economics:

   - _____, the desire to own something and the ability to pay for it
   - _____ curve, a graphic representation of a _____ schedule
   - _____ deposit, the money in checking accounts
   - _____ pull theory, the theory that inflation occurs when _____ for goods and services exceeds existing supplies
   - _____ schedule, a table that lists the quantity of a good a person will buy it each different price
   - _____ side economics, the school of economics at believes government spending and tax cuts open economy by raising _____

   a. McKesson ' Robbins scandal
   c. Variability
   b. Production
   d. Demand

6. In economics, _____ describes demand that is not very sensitive to a change in price.
   a. Export-led growth
   c. Effective unemployment rate
   b. Inflation hedge
   d. Inelastic

7. In economics, _____ is the ability of a firm to alter the market price of a good or service. A firm with _____ can raise prices without losing all customers to competitors.

   When a firm has _____ it faces a downward-sloping demand curve.

   a. Pacman conjecture
   c. Revenue-cap regulation
   b. Price makers
   d. Market power

8. _____ is a broad label that refers to any individuals or households that use goods and services generated within the economy. The concept of a _____ is used in different contexts, so that the usage and significance of the term may vary.

   Typically when business people and economists talk of _____s they are talking about person as _____, an aggregated commodity item with little individuality other than that expressed in the buy/not-buy decision.

   a. Consumer
   c. 130-30 fund
   b. 100-year flood
   d. 1921 recession

9. A _____ is a measure of the average price of consumer goods and services purchased by households. A _____ measures a price change for a constant market basket of goods and services from one period to the next within the same area (city, region, or nation.) It is a price index determined by measuring the price of a standard group of goods meant to represent the typical market basket of a typical urban consumer.
   a. Cost-of-living index
   c. Consumer Price Index
   b. CPI
   d. Lipstick index

Chapter 8. COMPETITION AND MONOPOLY

10. The _____ was an early English joint-stock company that was formed initially for pursuing trade with the East Indies, but that ended up trading with the Indian subcontinent and China. The oldest among several similarly formed European East India Companies, the Company was granted an English Royal Charter, under the name Governor and Company of Merchants of London Trading into the East Indies, by Elizabeth I on 31 December 1600. After a rival English company challenged its monopoly in the late 17th century, the two companies were merged in 1708 to form the United Company of Merchants of England Trading to the East Indies, commonly styled the Honourable _____, and abbreviated, HEast India Company; the Company was colloquially referred to as John Company, and in India as Company Bahadur .

   a. ACEA agreement
   b. AD-IA Model
   c. ACCRA Cost of Living Index
   d. East India Company

11. _____ in economics and business is the result of an exchange and from that trade we assign a numerical monetary value to a good, service or asset. If Alice trades Bob 4 apples for an orange, the _____ of an orange is 4 apples. Inversely, the _____ of an apple is 1/4 oranges.

   a. Price war
   b. Price book
   c. Premium pricing
   d. Price

12. A _____ is a normalized average (typically a weighted average) of prices for a given class of goods or services in a given region, during a given interval of time. It is a statistic designed to help to compare how these prices, taken as a whole, differ between time periods or geographical locations.

Price indices have several potential uses.

   a. Two-part tariff
   b. Product sabotage
   c. Transactional Net Margin Method
   d. Price Index

13. The _____ consists of a number of economic theories which describe the nature of the firm, company including its existence, its behaviour, and its relationship with the market.

In simplified terms, the _____ aims to answer these questions:

1. Existence - why do firms emerge, why are not all transactions in the economy mediated over the market?
2. Boundaries - why the boundary between firms and the market is located exactly there? Which transactions are performed internally and which are negotiated on the market?
3. Organization - why are firms structured in such specific way? What is the interplay of formal and informal relationships?

Despite looking simple, these questions are not answered by the established economic theory, which usually views firms as given, and treats them as black boxes without any internal structure.

The First World War period saw a change of emphasis in economic theory away from industry-level analysis which mainly included analysing markets to analysis at the level of the firm, as it became increasingly clear that perfect competition was no longer an adequate model of how firms behaved. Economic theory till then had focussed on trying to understand markets alone and there had been little study on understanding why firms or organisations exist.

Chapter 8. COMPETITION AND MONOPOLY

a. Khazzoom-Brookes postulate
c. Technology gap
b. Policy Ineffectiveness Proposition
d. Theory of the firm

14. Monopoly power is an example of market failure which occurs when one or more of the participants has the ability to influence the price or other outcomes in some general or specialized market. The most commonly discussed form of market power is that of a monopoly, but other forms such as monopsony, and more moderate versions of these two extremes, exist. Market participants that have market power are sometimes referred to as 'price makers', while those without are sometimes called '_____'.

a. Market concentration
c. Monopolization
b. Market power
d. Price takers

15. In economics, the _____ is the term used to refer to the environment in which bonds are bought and sold between a central bank ' its regulated banks. It is not a free market process.

- To intervene in the 'business cycle', a central bank may choose to go into the _____ and buy or sell government bonds, which is known as _____ operations to increase reserves.

a. Open Market
c. ACCRA Cost of Living Index
b. Outside money
d. Inside money

16. In economics, the _____ can be defined as the graph depicting the relationship between the price of a certain commodity, and the amount of it that consumers are willing and able to purchase at that given price. It is a graphic representation of a demand schedule. The _____ for all consumers together follows from the _____ of every individual consumer: the individual demands at each price are added together.

a. Wage curve
c. Kuznets curve
b. Cost curve
d. Demand curve

17. In economics, _____ is the difference between a company's total revenue and its opportunity costs. It is the increase in wealth that an investor has from making an investment, taking into consideration all costs associated with that investment including the opportunity cost of capital.

Profit is the factor income of the entrepreneur.

a. Economic profit
c. ACCRA Cost of Living Index
b. Accounting profit
d. Operating profit

18. In neoclassical economics and microeconomics, _____ describes the perfect being a market in which there are many small firms, all producing homogeneous goods. In the short term, such markets are productively inefficient as output will not occur where mc is equal to ac, but allocatively efficient, as output under _____ will always occur where mc is equal to mr, and therefore where mc equals ar. However, in the long term, such markets are both allocatively and productively efficient.

a. Perfect competition
c. Law of supply
b. Co-operative economics
d. General equilibrium

Chapter 8. COMPETITION AND MONOPOLY

19. _____ was a survey conducted by the U.S. Department of Justice to gauge the prevalence of alcohol and illegal drug use among prior arrestees. It was a reformulation of the prior Drug Use Forecasting (DUF) program, focused on five drugs in particular: cocaine, marijuana, methamphetamine, opiates, and PCP.

Participants were randomly selected from arrest records in major metropolitan areas; because no personally identifying information is taken from each record chosen, the resulting data can be correlated to arrest rates, but not to the total population of persons charged.

- a. ACEA agreement
- b. AD-IA Model
- c. ACCRA Cost of Living Index
- d. Arrestee Drug Abuse Monitoring

20. _____ was a Scottish moral philosopher and a pioneer of political economy. One of the key figures of the Scottish Enlightenment, Smith is the author of The Theory of Moral Sentiments and An Inquiry into the Nature and Causes of the Wealth of Nations. The latter, usually abbreviated as The Wealth of Nations, is considered his magnum opus and the first modern work of economics.

- a. Adam Smith
- b. Adolf Hitler
- c. Adolph Fischer
- d. Alan Greenspan

Chapter 9. PRICE SEARCHING

1. _____ is a broad label that refers to any individuals or households that use goods and services generated within the economy. The concept of a _____ is used in different contexts, so that the usage and significance of the term may vary.

Typically when business people and economists talk of _____s they are talking about person as _____, an aggregated commodity item with little individuality other than that expressed in the buy/not-buy decision.

- a. 1921 recession
- b. 130-30 fund
- c. 100-year flood
- d. Consumer

2. A _____ is a measure of the average price of consumer goods and services purchased by households. A _____ measures a price change for a constant market basket of goods and services from one period to the next within the same area (city, region, or nation.) It is a price index determined by measuring the price of a standard group of goods meant to represent the typical market basket of a typical urban consumer.
- a. Lipstick index
- b. CPI
- c. Cost-of-living index
- d. Consumer Price Index

3. _____ in economics and business is the result of an exchange and from that trade we assign a numerical monetary value to a good, service or asset. If Alice trades Bob 4 apples for an orange, the _____ of an orange is 4 apples. Inversely, the _____ of an apple is 1/4 oranges.
- a. Price book
- b. Price war
- c. Premium pricing
- d. Price

4. A _____ is a normalized average (typically a weighted average) of prices for a given class of goods or services in a given region, during a given interval of time. It is a statistic designed to help to compare how these prices, taken as a whole, differ between time periods or geographical locations.

Price indices have several potential uses.

- a. Product sabotage
- b. Two-part tariff
- c. Price Index
- d. Transactional Net Margin Method

5. In economics and finance, _____ is the change in total cost that arises when the quantity produced changes by one unit. It is the cost of producing one more unit of a good. Mathematically, the _____ function is expressed as the first derivative of the total cost (TC) function with respect to quantity (Q.)
- a. Quality costs
- b. Marginal cost
- c. Variable cost
- d. Khozraschyot

6. In microeconomics, _____ is the extra revenue that an additional unit of product will bring. It is the additional income from selling one more unit of a good; sometimes equal to price. It can also be described as the change in total revenue/change in number of units sold.
- a. Long term
- b. Reservation price
- c. Market demand schedule
- d. Marginal revenue

7. The term _____ was initially coined in 1989 by John Williamson to describe a set of ten specific economic policy prescriptions that he considered should constitute the 'standard' reform package promoted for crisis-wracked developing countries by Washington, DC-based institutions such as the International Monetary Fund (IMF), World Bank and the US Treasury Department.

Subsequently, as Williamson himself has pointed out, the term has come to be used in a different and broader sense, as a synonym for market fundamentalism; in this broader sense, Williamson states, it has been criticized by people such as George Soros and Nobel Laureate Joseph E. Stiglitz. The _____ is also criticized by others such as some Latin American politicians and heterodox economists.

- a. Secular basis
- b. Permanent income hypothesis
- c. Minimum wage
- d. Washington consensus

8. In economics, the _____ is the maximum amount a person would be willing to pay, sacrifice or exchange for a good.

Choice modelling techniques may be used to estimate the value of the _____ through a choice experiment.

- a. Round-tripping
- b. Global strategy
- c. Net pay
- d. Willingness to pay

9. The _____ is a group of three respected economists who advise the President of the United States on economic policy. It is a part of the Executive Office of the President of the United States, and provides much of the economic policy of the White House. The council prepares the annual Economic Report of the President.
- a. Constrained Pareto optimality
- b. Federal Reserve Bank Notes
- c. Hybrid renewable energy systems
- d. Council of Economic Advisers

10. _____s is the social science that studies the production, distribution, and consumption of goods and services. The term _____s comes from the Ancient Greek oá¼°κονομῖα from oá¼¶κος (oikos, 'house') + vŒµος (nomos, 'custom' or 'law'), hence 'rules of the house(hold)'. Current _____ models developed out of the broader field of political economy in the late 19th century, owing to a desire to use an empirical approach more akin to the physical sciences.
- a. Opportunity cost
- b. Energy economics
- c. Inflation
- d. Economic

11. Discounting is a financial mechanism in which a debtor obtains the right to delay payments to a creditor, for a defined period of time, in exchange for a charge or fee. Essentially, the party that owes money in the present purchases the right to delay the payment until some future date. The _____, or charge, is simply the difference between the original amount owed in the present and the amount that has to be paid in the future to settle the debt.
- a. Certified Risk Manager
- b. Reliability theory
- c. Reinsurance
- d. Discount

12. In finance, the term _____ describes various legal measures taken to ensure that debtors, whether individuals, businesses honor their debts and make an honest effort to repay the money that they owe. Generally regarded as a subdivision of tax law, _____ is most often enforced through a combination of audits and legal restrictions. For example, a provision of the Federal Debt Collection Procedure Act states that a person or organization indebted to the United States, against whom a judgment lien has been filed, is ineligible to receive a government grant.

Chapter 9. PRICE SEARCHING

a. Microcredit
c. Carryback loan
b. Hard money loan
d. Debt compliance

13. The _____ was a regulatory body in the United States created by the Interstate Commerce Act of 1887, which was signed into law by President Grover Cleveland. The agency was abolished in 1995, and the agency's remaining functions were transferred to the Surface Transportation Board.

The Commission's five members were appointed by the President with the consent of the United States Senate.

a. Interstate Commerce Commission
c. ACEA agreement
b. ACCRA Cost of Living Index
d. Office of Thrift Supervision

14. _____ exists when sales of identical goods or services are transacted at different prices from the same provider. In a theoretical market with perfect information, no transaction costs or prohibition on secondary exchange (or re-selling) to prevent arbitrage, _____ can only be a feature of monopoly and oligopoly markets, where market power can be exercised. Otherwise, the moment the seller tries to sell the same good at different prices, the buyer at the lower price can arbitrage by selling to the consumer buying at the higher price but with a tiny discount.

a. Lerner Index
c. Transfer pricing
b. Loss leader
d. Price discrimination

15. Economics:

- _____ ,the desire to own something and the ability to pay for it
- _____ curve,a graphic representation of a _____ schedule
- _____ deposit, the money in checking accounts
- _____ pull theory,the theory that inflation occurs when _____ for goods and services exceeds existing supplies
- _____ schedule,a table that lists the quantity of a good a person will buy it each different price
- _____ side economics,the school of economics at believes government spending and tax cuts open economy by raising _____

a. Variability
c. Demand
b. Production
d. McKesson ' Robbins scandal

16. _____ is one of the four Ps of the marketing mix. The other three aspects are product, promotion, and place. It is also a key variable in microeconomic price allocation theory.

a. Point of total assumption
c. Guaranteed Maximum Price
b. Premium pricing
d. Pricing

Chapter 10. COMPETITION AND GOVERNMENT POLICY

1. The phrase _____ and acquisitions refers to the aspect of corporate strategy, corporate finance and management dealing with the buying, selling and combining of different companies that can aid, finance, or help a growing company in a given industry grow rapidly without having to create another business entity.

An acquisition, also known as a takeover or a buyout, is the buying of one company (the 'target') by another. An acquisition may be friendly or hostile.

- a. Differential accumulation
- b. Mergers
- c. Peace dividend
- d. Political economy

2. _____ was a survey conducted by the U.S. Department of Justice to gauge the prevalence of alcohol and illegal drug use among prior arrestees. It was a reformulation of the prior Drug Use Forecasting (DUF) program, focused on five drugs in particular: cocaine, marijuana, methamphetamine, opiates, and PCP.

Participants were randomly selected from arrest records in major metropolitan areas; because no personally identifying information is taken from each record chosen, the resulting data can be correlated to arrest rates, but not to the total population of persons charged.

- a. ACCRA Cost of Living Index
- b. ACEA agreement
- c. AD-IA Model
- d. Arrestee Drug Abuse Monitoring

3. _____ is an economic system in which wealth, and the means of producing wealth, are privately owned. Through _____, the land, labor, and capital are owned, operated, and traded for the purpose of generating profits, without force or fraud, by private individuals either singly or jointly, and investments, distribution, income, production, pricing and supply of goods, commodities and services are determined by voluntary private decision in a market economy. A distinguishing feature of _____ is that each person owns his or her own labor and therefore is allowed to sell the use of it to employers.

- a. Socialism for the rich and capitalism for the poor
- b. Capitalism
- c. Late capitalism
- d. Creative capitalism

4. _____ was a Scottish moral philosopher and a pioneer of political economy. One of the key figures of the Scottish Enlightenment, Smith is the author of The Theory of Moral Sentiments and An Inquiry into the Nature and Causes of the Wealth of Nations. The latter, usually abbreviated as The Wealth of Nations, is considered his magnum opus and the first modern work of economics.

- a. Alan Greenspan
- b. Adolf Hitler
- c. Adolph Fischer
- d. Adam Smith

5. An Inquiry into the Nature and Causes of the _____ is the magnum opus of the Scottish economist Adam Smith. It is a clearly written account of economics at the dawn of the Industrial Revolution, as well as a rhetorical piece written for the generally educated individual of the 18th century - advocating a free market economy as more productive and more beneficial to society.

The work is credited as a watershed in history and economics due to its comprehensive, largely accurate characterization of economic mechanisms that survive in modern economics; and also for its effective use of rhetorical technique, including structuring the work to contrast real world examples of free and fettered markets.

Chapter 10. COMPETITION AND GOVERNMENT POLICY

a. Wealth of Nations
b. Black Book of Communism
c. The Bell Curve
d. The Rise and Fall of the Great Powers

6. A _____ is a counterfeit agreement among industries. It is an informal organization of producers that agree to coordinate prices and production. _____s usually occur in an oligopolistic industry, where there is a small number of sellers and usually involve homogeneous products.
   a. Shanzhai
   b. Shill
   c. 100-year flood
   d. Cartel

7. _____ is the transition of a national economy from monopoly control by groups of large businesses to a free market economy. This change rarely arises naturally, and is generally the result of regulation by a governing body.

A modern example of _____ is the economic restructuring of Germany after the fall of the Third Reich in 1945.

   a. Monopolization
   b. Decartelization
   c. Complementary monopoly
   d. Market power

8. In economics and sociology, an _____ is any factor (financial or non-financial) that enables or motivates a particular course of action, or counts as a reason for preferring one choice to the alternatives. It is an expectation that encourages people to behave in a certain way. Since human beings are purposeful creatures, the study of _____ structures is central to the study of all economic activity (both in terms of individual decision-making and in terms of co-operation and competition within a larger institutional structure.)
   a. Economic reform
   b. Isocost
   c. Epstein-Zin preferences
   d. Incentive

9. _____ is a broad label that refers to any individuals or households that use goods and services generated within the economy. The concept of a _____ is used in different contexts, so that the usage and significance of the term may vary.

Typically when business people and economists talk of _____s they are talking about person as _____, an aggregated commodity item with little individuality other than that expressed in the buy/not-buy decision.

   a. 1921 recession
   b. 130-30 fund
   c. 100-year flood
   d. Consumer

10. A _____ is a measure of the average price of consumer goods and services purchased by households. A _____ measures a price change for a constant market basket of goods and services from one period to the next within the same area (city, region, or nation.) It is a price index determined by measuring the price of a standard group of goods meant to represent the typical market basket of a typical urban consumer.
    a. CPI
    b. Lipstick index
    c. Cost-of-living index
    d. Consumer Price Index

Chapter 10. COMPETITION AND GOVERNMENT POLICY

11. _____ in economics and business is the result of an exchange and from that trade we assign a numerical monetary value to a good, service or asset. If Alice trades Bob 4 apples for an orange, the _____ of an orange is 4 apples. Inversely, the _____ of an apple is 1/4 oranges.
   a. Premium pricing
   b. Price book
   c. Price
   d. Price war

12. A _____ is a normalized average (typically a weighted average) of prices for a given class of goods or services in a given region, during a given interval of time. It is a statistic designed to help to compare how these prices, taken as a whole, differ between time periods or geographical locations.

   Price indices have several potential uses.

   a. Two-part tariff
   b. Price Index
   c. Transactional Net Margin Method
   d. Product sabotage

13. A _____ occurs when an entity spends more money than it takes in. The opposite of a _____ is a budget surplus. Debt is essentially an accumulated flow of deficits.
   a. Public Financial Management
   b. Budget deficit
   c. Funding body
   d. Lump-sum tax

14. The _____ was a regulatory body in the United States created by the Interstate Commerce Act of 1887, which was signed into law by President Grover Cleveland. The agency was abolished in 1995, and the agency's remaining functions were transferred to the Surface Transportation Board.

   The Commission's five members were appointed by the President with the consent of the United States Senate.

   a. ACCRA Cost of Living Index
   b. Interstate Commerce Commission
   c. Office of Thrift Supervision
   d. ACEA agreement

15. The _____ is a group of three respected economists who advise the President of the United States on economic policy. It is a part of the Executive Office of the President of the United States, and provides much of the economic policy of the White House. The council prepares the annual Economic Report of the President.
   a. Hybrid renewable energy systems
   b. Council of Economic Advisers
   c. Federal Reserve Bank Notes
   d. Constrained Pareto optimality

16. _____s is the social science that studies the production, distribution, and consumption of goods and services. The term _____s comes from the Ancient Greek oá¼°κονομῖα from oá¼¶κος (oikos, 'house') + vÏŒμος (nomos, 'custom' or 'law'), hence 'rules of the house(hold)'. Current _____ models developed out of the broader field of political economy in the late 19th century, owing to a desire to use an empirical approach more akin to the physical sciences.
   a. Inflation
   b. Opportunity cost
   c. Economic
   d. Energy economics

17. _____ is a process of attributing cost to particular cost centres. For example the wage of the driver of the purchasing department can be allocated to the purchasing department cost centre. It is not necessary to share the wage cost over several different cost centers.

Chapter 10. COMPETITION AND GOVERNMENT POLICY

a. Marginal cost
c. Repugnancy costs

b. Quality costs
d. Cost allocation

18. In economics and business decision-making, _____ are costs that cannot be recovered once they have been incurred. _____ are sometimes contrasted with variable costs, which are the costs that will change due to the proposed course of action, and prospective costs which are costs that will be incurred if an action is taken.

In traditional microeconomic theory, only variable costs are relevant to a decision.

a. Hyperbolic discounting
c. Halo effect

b. Post-purchase rationalization
d. Sunk costs

19. _____ is a voluntary transfer of resources from one country to another, given at least partly with the objective of benefiting the recipient country. It may have other functions as well: it may be given as a signal of diplomatic approval, or to strengthen a military ally, to reward a government for behaviour desired by the donor, to extend the donor's cultural influence, to provide infrastructure needed by the donor for resource extraction from the recipient country, or to gain other kinds of commercial access. Humanitarianism and altruism are, nevertheless, significant motivations for the giving of _____.

a. Aid
c. ACCRA Cost of Living Index

b. AD-IA Model
d. ACEA agreement

20. _____ was a federal assistance program in effect from 1935 to 1997, which was administered by the United States Department of Health and Human Services. This program provided financial assistance to children whose families had low or no income.

The program was created under the name Aid to Dependent Children (ADC) by the Social Security Act of 1935 as part of the New Deal; the words 'families with' were added to the name in 1960, partly due to concern that the program's rules discouraged marriage.

a. AD-IA Model
c. ACCRA Cost of Living Index

b. ACEA agreement
d. Aid to Families with Dependent Children

21. Competition law, known in the United States as _____ law, has three main elements:

- prohibiting agreements or practices that restrict free trading and competition between business entities. This includes in particular the repression of cartels.
- banning abusive behaviour by a firm dominating a market, or anti-competitive practices that tend to lead to such a dominant position. Practices controlled in this way may include predatory pricing, tying, price gouging, refusal to deal, and many others.
- supervising the mergers and acquisitions of large corporations, including some joint ventures. Transactions that are considered to threaten the competitive process can be prohibited altogether, or approved subject to 'remedies' such as an obligation to divest part of the merged business or to offer licences or access to facilities to enable other businesses to continue competing.

Chapter 10. COMPETITION AND GOVERNMENT POLICY

The substance and practice of competition law varies from jurisdiction to jurisdiction. Protecting the interests of consumers (consumer welfare) and ensuring that entrepreneurs have an opportunity to compete in the market economy are often treated as important objectives. Competition law is closely connected with law on deregulation of access to markets, state aids and subsidies, the privatisation of state owned assets and the establishment of independent sector regulators. In recent decades, competition law has been viewed as a way to provide better public services.

a. United Kingdom competition law
b. Intellectual property law
c. Antitrust
d. Anti-Inflation Act

22. The _____ is the apparent contradiction that although water is on the whole more useful, in terms of survival, than diamonds, diamonds command a higher price in the market. The economist Adam Smith is often considered to be the classic presenter of this paradox. Nicolaus Copernicus, John Locke, John Law and others had previously tried to explain the disparity.

a. 100-year flood
b. 130-30 fund
c. St. Petersburg paradox
d. Paradox of value

23.

The _____ was the first United States Federal statute to limit cartels and monopolies. It falls under antitrust law.

The Act provides: 'Every contract, combination in the form of trust or otherwise, or conspiracy, in restraint of trade or commerce among the several States, or with foreign nations, is declared to be illegal'. The Act also provides: 'Every person who shall monopolize, or attempt to monopolize, or combine or conspire with any other person or persons, to monopolize any part of the trade or commerce among the several States, or with foreign nations, shall be deemed guilty of a felony [. . .]' The Act put responsibility upon government attorneys and district courts to pursue and investigate trusts, companies and organizations suspected of violating the Act. The Clayton Act extended the right to sue under the antitrust laws to 'any person who shall be injured in his business or property by reason of anything forbidden in the antitrust laws.' Under the Clayton Act, private parties may sue in U.S. district court and should they prevail, they may be awarded treble damages and the cost of suit, including reasonable attorney's fees.

a. 100-year flood
b. 130-30 fund
c. 1921 recession
d. Sherman Antitrust Act

24. _____ is the removal or simplification of government rules and regulations that constrain the operation of market forces. _____ does not mean elimination of laws against fraud, but eliminating or reducing government control of how business is done, thereby moving toward a more free market.

The stated rationale for '_____' is often that fewer and simpler regulations will lead to a raised level of competitiveness, therefore higher productivity, more efficiency and lower prices overall.

Chapter 10. COMPETITION AND GOVERNMENT POLICY

a. Secular basis
b. Deregulation
c. Macroeconomic policy instruments
d. Fundamental psychological law

25. In finance, the term _____ describes various legal measures taken to ensure that debtors, whether individuals, businesses honor their debts and make an honest effort to repay the money that they owe. Generally regarded as a subdivision of tax law, _____ is most often enforced through a combination of audits and legal restrictions. For example, a provision of the Federal Debt Collection Procedure Act states that a person or organization indebted to the United States, against whom a judgment lien has been filed, is ineligible to receive a government grant.
   a. Microcredit
   b. Hard money loan
   c. Carryback loan
   d. Debt compliance

26. The _____ is an independent agency of the United States government, established in 1914 by the _____ Act. Its principal mission is the promotion of 'consumer protection' and the elimination and prevention of what regulators perceive to be harmfully 'anti-competitive' business practices, such as coercive monopoly.

The _____ Act was one of President Wilson's major acts against trusts.

   a. 100-year flood
   b. 130-30 fund
   c. 1921 recession
   d. Federal Trade Commission

27. The _____ of 1914 (15 U.S.C §§ 41-58, as amended) established the Federal Trade Commission (FTC), a bipartisan body of five members appointed by the President of the United States for seven year terms. This Commission was authorized to issue Cease and Desist orders to large corporations to curb unfair trade practices. This Act also gave more flexibility to the US congress for judicial matters.
   a. Competition law theory
   b. Minimum wage law
   c. Buydown
   d. Federal Trade Commission Act

28. A _____ is officially defined as being 'any merger that is not horizontal or vertical; in general, it is the combination of firms in different industries or firms operating in different geographic areas'. _____s can serve various purposes, including extending corporate territories and extending a product range. One example of a _____ was the merger between the Walt Disney Company and the American Broadcasting Company.
   a. Borrowing base
   b. Factor cost
   c. Cost-effectiveness analysis
   d. Conglomerate merger

29. The _____ or gross domestic income (GDI), a basic measure of an economy's economic performance, is the market value of all final goods and services produced within the borders of a nation in a year. _____ can be defined in three ways, all of which are conceptually identical. First, it is equal to the total expenditures for all final goods and services produced within the country in a stipulated period of time (usually a 365-day year.)
   a. Countercyclical
   b. Gross domestic product
   c. Market structure
   d. Monopolistic competition

30. In economics, a _____ is the combination of two or more firms competing in the same market with the same good or service.See Horizontal integration.
   a. Financial system
   b. Horizontal merger
   c. Federal Reserve districts
   d. Market dominance

Chapter 10. COMPETITION AND GOVERNMENT POLICY

31. _____ is a misspelled phrase from Latin 'pro capite' phrase meaning per head with pro meaning 'per' or 'for each' and capite meaning 'head.' Both words together equate to the phrase 'for each head.'

It is usually used in the field of statistics to indicate the average per person for any given concern, such as income, crime rate, etc.

It is also used in wills to indicate that each of the named beneficiaries should receive, by devise or bequest, equal shares of the estate. This is in contrast to a per stirpes division, in which each branch of the inheriting family inherits an equal share of the estate.

- a. Population statistics
- b. False positive rate
- c. Sargan test
- d. Per capita

32. False advertising or _____ is the use of false or misleading statements in advertising. As advertising has the potential to persuade people into commercial transactions that they might otherwise avoid, many governments around the world use regulations to control false, deceptive or misleading advertising. Truth in labeling refers to essentially the same concept, that customers have the right to know what they are buying, and that all necessary information should be on the label.

- a. 100-year flood
- b. 130-30 fund
- c. Deceptive advertising
- d. 1921 recession

33. _____ is a fee paid on borrowed assets. It is the price paid for the use of borrowed money, or, money earned by deposited funds. Assets that are sometimes lent with _____ include money, shares, consumer goods through hire purchase, major assets such as aircraft, and even entire factories in finance lease arrangements.

- a. Internal debt
- b. Insolvency
- c. Asset protection
- d. Interest

34. An _____ is a market form in which a market or industry is dominated by a small number of sellers (oligopolists.) Because there are few participants in this type of market, each oligopolist is aware of the actions of the others. The decisions of one firm influence, and are influenced by, the decisions of other firms.

- a. Oligopsony
- b. ACEA agreement
- c. Oligopoly
- d. ACCRA Cost of Living Index

35. In marketing, _____ is the process of distinguishing the differences of a product or offering from others, to make it more attractive to a particular target market. This involves differentiating it from competitors' products as well as one's own product offerings.

Differentiation is a source of competitive advantage.

- a. Market segment
- b. Product differentiation
- c. Pricing science
- d. Technology acceptance model

36. The _____ of 1980, signed into law by President Jimmy Carter on October 14, deregulated the railroad industry (to a significant extent) and replaced the regulatory structure that existed since the 1887 Interstate Commerce Act.

This Act followed the Railroad Revitalization and Regulatory Reform Act of 1976, which established the basic outlines of regulatory reform in the railroad industry -- greater range for railroad pricing without close regulatory restraint, greater independence from collective rate making procedures in rail pricing and service offers, contract rates, and, to a lesser extent, greater freedom for entry into and exit from rail markets.

Though the '4R' Act established these guidelines, the Interstate Commerce Commission at first did not give much effect to its legislative mandates.

a. 130-30 fund
c. 100-year flood

b. Staggers Rail Act
d. 1921 recession

Chapter 11. THE DISTRIBUTION OF INCOME

1. _____ was a survey conducted by the U.S. Department of Justice to gauge the prevalence of alcohol and illegal drug use among prior arrestees. It was a reformulation of the prior Drug Use Forecasting (DUF) program, focused on five drugs in particular: cocaine, marijuana, methamphetamine, opiates, and PCP.

Participants were randomly selected from arrest records in major metropolitan areas; because no personally identifying information is taken from each record chosen, the resulting data can be correlated to arrest rates, but not to the total population of persons charged.

   a. ACEA agreement
   b. AD-IA Model
   c. ACCRA Cost of Living Index
   d. Arrestee Drug Abuse Monitoring

2. In economics, the _____ is a historical inverse relation between the rate of unemployment and the rate of inflation in an economy. Stated simply, the lower the unemployment in an economy, the higher the rate of increase in nominal wages in the economy. Rate of Change of Wages against Unemployment, United Kingdom 1913-1948 from Phillips (1958)

William Phillips, a New Zealand born economist, wrote a paper in 1958 titled The Relationship between Unemployment and the Rate of Change of Money Wages in the United Kingdom 1861-1957, which was published in the quarterly journal Economica.

   a. Lorenz curve
   b. Demand curve
   c. Phillips curve
   d. Cost curve

3. _____ was a Scottish moral philosopher and a pioneer of political economy. One of the key figures of the Scottish Enlightenment, Smith is the author of The Theory of Moral Sentiments and An Inquiry into the Nature and Causes of the Wealth of Nations. The latter, usually abbreviated as The Wealth of Nations, is considered his magnum opus and the first modern work of economics.

   a. Adam Smith
   b. Alan Greenspan
   c. Adolf Hitler
   d. Adolph Fischer

4. An Inquiry into the Nature and Causes of the _____ is the magnum opus of the Scottish economist Adam Smith. It is a clearly written account of economics at the dawn of the Industrial Revolution, as well as a rhetorical piece written for the generally educated individual of the 18th century - advocating a free market economy as more productive and more beneficial to society.

The work is credited as a watershed in history and economics due to its comprehensive, largely accurate characterization of economic mechanisms that survive in modern economics; and also for its effective use of rhetorical technique, including structuring the work to contrast real world examples of free and fettered markets.

   a. The Bell Curve
   b. Black Book of Communism
   c. Wealth of Nations
   d. The Rise and Fall of the Great Powers

Chapter 11. THE DISTRIBUTION OF INCOME

5. Economics:

   - _____, the desire to own something and the ability to pay for it
   - _____ curve, a graphic representation of a _____ schedule
   - _____ deposit, the money in checking accounts
   - _____ pull theory, the theory that inflation occurs when _____ for goods and services exceeds existing supplies
   - _____ schedule, a table that lists the quantity of a good a person will buy it each different price
   - _____ side economics, the school of economics at believes government spending and tax cuts open economy by raising _____

   a. McKesson ' Robbins scandal   b. Demand
   c. Variability   d. Production

6. In economics, _____ is how a natione;s total economy is distributed among its population. ._____ has always been a central concern of economic theory and economic policy. Classical economists such as Adam Smith, Thomas Malthus and David Ricardo were mainly concerned with factor _____, that is, the distribution of income between the main factors of production, land, labour and capital.

   a. Income distribution   b. Eco commerce
   c. Authorised capital   d. Equipment trust certificate

7. _____ is an economic model based on price, utility and quantity in a market. It predicts that in a competitive market, price will function to equalize the quantity demanded by consumers, and the quantity supplied by producers, resulting in an economic equilibrium of price and quantity. The model incorporates other factors changing equilibrium as a shift of demand and/or supply.

   a. Deferred gratification   b. Supply and demand
   c. Joint demand   d. Rational addiction

8. _____ is an online peer-reviewed magazine published by the Agricultural ' Applied Economics Association (AAEA) for readers interested in the policy and management of agriculture, the food industry, natural resources, rural communities, and the environment. _____ is published quarterly and is available free online. It is currently one of three outreach products offered by AAEA, along with the more timely Policy Issues and the forthcoming Shared Materials section of the AAEA Web site.

   a. 1921 recession   b. Choices
   c. 100-year flood   d. 130-30 fund

9. _____ is a fee paid on borrowed assets. It is the price paid for the use of borrowed money , or, money earned by deposited funds . Assets that are sometimes lent with _____ include money, shares, consumer goods through hire purchase, major assets such as aircraft, and even entire factories in finance lease arrangements.

   a. Internal debt   b. Asset protection
   c. Insolvency   d. Interest

10. The _____ was a regulatory body in the United States created by the Interstate Commerce Act of 1887, which was signed into law by President Grover Cleveland. The agency was abolished in 1995, and the agency's remaining functions were transferred to the Surface Transportation Board.

The Commission's five members were appointed by the President with the consent of the United States Senate.

a. ACEA agreement
b. Office of Thrift Supervision
c. ACCRA Cost of Living Index
d. Interstate Commerce Commission

11. _____ refers to the stock of skills and knowledge embodied in the ability to perform labor so as to produce economic value. It is the skills and knowledge gained by a worker through education and experience. Many early economic theories refer to it simply as labor, one of three factors of production, and consider it to be a fungible resource -- homogeneous and easily interchangeable. Other conceptions of labor dispense with these assumptions.

a. Law of increasing costs
b. General equilibrium
c. Price theory
d. Human capital

12. In mathematics, an _____ is a statement about the relative size or order of two objects, or about whether they are the same or not

- The notation a < b means that a is less than b.
- The notation a > b means that a is greater than b.
- The notation a ≠ b means that a is not equal to b, but does not say that one is greater than the other or even that they can be compared in size.

In each statement above, a is not equal to b. These relations are known as strict inequalities. The notation a < b may also be read as 'a is strictly less than b'.

a. Inequality
b. AD-IA Model
c. ACCRA Cost of Living Index
d. ACEA agreement

13. A _____ is the exclusive authority to determine how a resource is used, whether that resource is owned by government or by individuals. All economic goods have a _____s attribute. This attribute has three broad components

1. The right to use the good
2. The right to earn income from the good
3. The right to transfer the good to others

The concept of _____s as used by economists and legal scholars are related but distinct. The distinction is largely seen in the economists' focus on the ability of an individual or collective to control the use of the good.

a. Post-sale restraint
b. High-reeve
c. Holder in due course
d. Property right

14. Economic _____ is defined as an excess distribution to any factor in a production process above that which is required to induce the factor into the process or any excess above that which is necessary to keep the factor in its current use..

Chapter 11. THE DISTRIBUTION OF INCOME

Classical Factor _____ is primarily concerned with the fee paid for the use of fixed (e.g. natural) resources. The classical definition is expressed as any excess payment above that required to induce or provide for production.

- a. 100-year flood
- b. 1921 recession
- c. Rent
- d. 130-30 fund

15. _____ refers to laws or ordinances that set price controls on the renting of residential housing. It functions as a price ceiling.

_____ exists in approximately 40 countries around the world.

- a. Tenant rights
- b. National Housing Conference
- c. 100-year flood
- d. Rent control

16. _____ is sometimes referred to as _____, actually it means Economic Monetary Union.

First ideas of an economic and monetary union in Europe were raised well before establishing the European Communities. For example, already in the League of Nations, Gustav Stresemann asked in 1929 for a European currency (Link) against the background of an increased economic division due to a number of new nation states in Europe after WWI.

- a. European Monetary Union
- b. Exchange rate mechanism
- c. Euro Interbank Offered Rate
- d. European Monetary System

17. An economic and _____ is a single market with a common currency. It is to be distinguished from a mere currency union, which does not involve a single market. This is the fifth stage of economic integration.
- a. Monetary Union
- b. Commercial invoice
- c. Free trade zone
- d. Customs union

18. The accounting equation relates assets, _____, and owner's equity:

   Assets = _____ + Owner's Equity

The accounting equation is the mathematical structure of the balance sheet.

The Australian Accounting Research Foundation defines _____ as: 'future sacrifice of economic benefits that the entity is presently obliged to make to other entities as a result of past transactions and other past events.'

Probably the most accepted accounting definition of liability is the one used by the International Accounting Standards Board (IASB.) The following is a quotation from IFRS Framework:

A liability is a present obligation of the enterprise arising from past events, the settlement of which is expected to result in an outflow from the enterprise of resources embodying economic benefits

Chapter 11. THE DISTRIBUTION OF INCOME

Regulations as to the recognition of _____ are different all over the world, but are roughly similar to those of the IASB.

a. Community property
b. Coase theorem
c. Competition law theory
d. Liabilities

19. In economics and finance, _____ is the change in total cost that arises when the quantity produced changes by one unit. It is the cost of producing one more unit of a good. Mathematically, the _____ function is expressed as the first derivative of the total cost (TC) function with respect to quantity (Q.)

a. Marginal cost
b. Khozraschyot
c. Quality costs
d. Variable cost

20. In microeconomics, _____ is the extra revenue that an additional unit of product will bring. It is the additional income from selling one more unit of a good; sometimes equal to price. It can also be described as the change in total revenue/change in number of units sold.

a. Long term
b. Marginal revenue
c. Market demand schedule
d. Reservation price

21. _____ is a term in economics, where demand for one good or service occurs as a result of demand for another. This may occur as the former is a part of production of the second. For example, demand for coal leads to _____ for mining, as coal must be mined for coal to be consumed.

a. Days Sales Outstanding
b. Derived demand
c. Leontief production function
d. Rate risk

22. In finance, the term _____ describes various legal measures taken to ensure that debtors, whether individuals, businesses honor their debts and make an honest effort to repay the money that they owe. Generally regarded as a subdivision of tax law, _____ is most often enforced through a combination of audits and legal restrictions. For example, a provision of the Federal Debt Collection Procedure Act states that a person or organization indebted to the United States, against whom a judgment lien has been filed, is ineligible to receive a government grant.

a. Debt compliance
b. Hard money loan
c. Microcredit
d. Carryback loan

23. _____ is an economic system in which wealth, and the means of producing wealth, are privately owned. Through _____, the land, labor, and capital are owned, operated, and traded for the purpose of generating profits, without force or fraud, by private individuals either singly or jointly, and investments, distribution, income, production, pricing and supply of goods, commodities and services are determined by voluntary private decision in a market economy. A distinguishing feature of _____ is that each person owns his or her own labor and therefore is allowed to sell the use of it to employers.

a. Socialism for the rich and capitalism for the poor
b. Creative capitalism
c. Late capitalism
d. Capitalism

24. A _____ is a counterfeit agreement among industries. It is an informal organization of producers that agree to coordinate prices and production. _____s usually occur in an oligopolistic industry, where there is a small number of sellers and usually involve homogeneous products.

a. 100-year flood	b. Shill
c. Shanzhai	d. Cartel

25. _____ is the transition of a national economy from monopoly control by groups of large businesses to a free market economy. This change rarely arises naturally, and is generally the result of regulation by a governing body.

A modern example of _____ is the economic restructuring of Germany after the fall of the Third Reich in 1945.

- a. Market power
- b. Monopolization
- c. Decartelization
- d. Complementary monopoly

26. A _____ or labor union is an organization of workers who have banded together to achieve common goals in key areas and working conditions. The _____, through its leadership, bargains with the employer on behalf of union members (rank and file members) and negotiates labor contracts (Collective bargaining) with employers. This may include the negotiation of wages, work rules, complaint procedures, rules governing hiring, firing and promotion of workers, benefits, workplace safety and policies.

- a. Consumer goods
- b. Case-Shiller Home Price Indices
- c. Guaranteed investment contracts
- d. Trade union

27. _____s is the social science that studies the production, distribution, and consumption of goods and services. The term _____s comes from the Ancient Greek oá¼°κονομῖα from oá¼¶κος (oikos, 'house') + vÏŒμος (nomos, 'custom' or 'law'), hence 'rules of the house(hold)'. Current _____ models developed out of the broader field of political economy in the late 19th century, owing to a desire to use an empirical approach more akin to the physical sciences.

- a. Inflation
- b. Energy economics
- c. Opportunity cost
- d. Economic

28. A _____ is the lowest hourly, daily or monthly wage that employers may legally pay to employees or workers. Equivalently, it is the lowest wage at which workers may sell their labor. Although _____ laws are in effect in a great many jurisdictions, there are differences of opinion about the benefits and drawbacks of a _____.

- a. Microfoundations
- b. Minimum wage
- c. Marginal propensity to consume
- d. Permanent war economy

29. _____ is the shortage of common things such as food, clothing, shelter and safe drinking water, all of which determine the quality of life. It may also include the lack of access to opportunities such as education and employment which aid the escape from _____ and/or allow one to enjoy the respect of fellow citizens. According to Mollie Orshansky who developed the _____ measurements used by the U.S. government, 'to be poor is to be deprived of those goods and services and pleasures which others around us take for granted.' Ongoing debates over causes, effects and best ways to measure _____, directly influence the design and implementation of _____-reduction programs and are therefore relevant to the fields of public administration and international development.

- a. Liberal welfare reforms
- b. Poverty map
- c. Growth Elasticity of Poverty
- d. Poverty

Chapter 11. THE DISTRIBUTION OF INCOME

30. _____ is a voluntary transfer of resources from one country to another, given at least partly with the objective of benefiting the recipient country. It may have other functions as well: it may be given as a signal of diplomatic approval, or to strengthen a military ally, to reward a government for behaviour desired by the donor, to extend the donor's cultural influence, to provide infrastructure needed by the donor for resource extraction from the recipient country, or to gain other kinds of commercial access. Humanitarianism and altruism are, nevertheless, significant motivations for the giving of _____.
    a. ACEA agreement
    b. AD-IA Model
    c. Aid
    d. ACCRA Cost of Living Index

31. _____ was a federal assistance program in effect from 1935 to 1997, which was administered by the United States Department of Health and Human Services. This program provided financial assistance to children whose families had low or no income.

The program was created under the name Aid to Dependent Children (ADC) by the Social Security Act of 1935 as part of the New Deal; the words 'families with' were added to the name in 1960, partly due to concern that the program's rules discouraged marriage.

    a. ACEA agreement
    b. AD-IA Model
    c. ACCRA Cost of Living Index
    d. Aid to Families with Dependent Children

32. _____ is the United States of America's federal assistance program, formerly known as 'welfare'. It began on July 1, 1997, and succeeded the Aid to Families with Dependent Children program, providing cash assistance to indigent American families with dependent children through the United States Department of Health and Human Services. Prior to 1997, the federal government designed the overall program requirements and guidelines, while states administered the program and determined eligibility for benefits.
    a. 1921 recession
    b. 100-year flood
    c. 130-30 fund
    d. Temporary Assistance for Needy Families

33. The _____ is the minimum level of income deemed necessary to achieve an adequate standard of living in a given country. In practice, like the definition of poverty, the official or common understanding of the poverty line is significantly higher in developed countries than in developing countries.

The common international poverty line has been roughly $1 a day, or more precisely $1.08 at 1993 purchasing-power parity (PPP.)

    a. Poverty
    b. Poverty map
    c. Poverty threshold
    d. Poverty reduction

34. To _____ is to impose a financial charge or other levy upon a taxpayer by a state or the functional equivalent of a state.

_____es are also imposed by many subnational entities. _____es consist of direct _____ or indirect _____, and may be paid in money or as its labour equivalent (often but not always unpaid.)

    a. Tax
    b. 1921 recession
    c. 100-year flood
    d. 130-30 fund

Chapter 11. THE DISTRIBUTION OF INCOME 83

35. A _____ is:

- Rewrite _____, in generative grammar and computer science
- Standardization, a formal and widely-accepted statement, fact, definition, or qualification
- Operation, a determinate _____ for performing a mathematical operation and obtaining a certain result (Mathematics, Logic)
    - Unary operation
    - Binary operation
- _____ of inference, a function from sets of formulae to formulae (Mathematics, Logic)
- _____ of thumb, principle with broad application that is not intended to be strictly accurate or reliable for every situation. Also often simply referred to as a _____
- Moral, an atomic element of a moral code for guiding choices in human behavior
- Heuristic, a quantized '_____' which shows a tendency or probability for successful function
- A regulation, as in sports
- A Production _____, as in computer science
- Procedural law, a _____ set governing the application of laws to cases
    - A law, which may informally be called a '_____'
    - A court ruling, a decision by a court
- In the U.S. Government, a regulation mandated by Congress, but written or expanded upon by the Executive Branch.
- Norm (sociology), an informal but widely accepted _____, concept, truth, definition, or qualification (social norms, legal norms, coding norms)
- Norm (philosophy), a kind of sentence or a reason to act, feel or believe
- 'Rulership' is the concept of governance by a government:
    - Military _____, governance by a military body
    - Monastic _____, a collection of precepts that guides the life of monks or nuns in a religious order where the superior holds the place of Christ
- Slide _____

- '_____,' a song by Ayumi Hamasaki
- '_____,' a song by rapper Nas
- '_____s,' an album by the band The Whitest Boy Alive
- _____s: Pyaar Ka Superhit Formula, a 2003 Bollywood film
- ruler, an instrument for measuring lengths
- _____, a component of an astrolabe, circumferator or similar instrument
- The _____s, a bestselling self-help book
- _____ Project (Run Up-to-date Linux Everywhere), a project that aims to use up-to-date Linux software on old PCs
- _____ engine, a software system that helps managing business _____s
- Ja _____, a hip hop artist
    - R.U.L.E., a 2005 greatest hits album by rapper Ja _____
- '_____s,' a KMFDM song

a. Demand	b. Technocracy
c. Procter ' Gamble	d. Rule

Chapter 12. EXTERNALITIES AND CONFLICTING RIGHTS

1. _____ is a broad label that refers to any individuals or households that use goods and services generated within the economy. The concept of a _____ is used in different contexts, so that the usage and significance of the term may vary.

Typically when business people and economists talk of _____s they are talking about person as _____, an aggregated commodity item with little individuality other than that expressed in the buy/not-buy decision.

   a. Consumer
   b. 1921 recession
   c. 100-year flood
   d. 130-30 fund

2. A _____ is a measure of the average price of consumer goods and services purchased by households. A _____ measures a price change for a constant market basket of goods and services from one period to the next within the same area (city, region, or nation.) It is a price index determined by measuring the price of a standard group of goods meant to represent the typical market basket of a typical urban consumer.
   a. Consumer Price Index
   b. Lipstick index
   c. CPI
   d. Cost-of-living index

3. _____ is sometimes referred to as _____, actually it means Economic Monetary Union.

First ideas of an economic and monetary union in Europe were raised well before establishing the European Communities. For example, already in the League of Nations, Gustav Stresemann asked in 1929 for a European currency (Link) against the background of an increased economic division due to a number of new nation states in Europe after WWI.

   a. Euro Interbank Offered Rate
   b. Exchange rate mechanism
   c. European Monetary System
   d. European Monetary Union

4. An economic and _____ is a single market with a common currency. It is to be distinguished from a mere currency union , which does not involve a single market. This is the fifth stage of economic integration.
   a. Free trade zone
   b. Customs union
   c. Commercial invoice
   d. Monetary Union

5. _____s (economically referred to as land or raw materials) occur naturally within environments that exist relatively undisturbed by mankind, in a natural form. A _____'s is often characterized by amounts of biodiversity existent in various ecosystems.

Mining, petroleum extraction, fishing, hunting, and forestry are generally considered natural-resource industries.

   a. 100-year flood
   b. 1921 recession
   c. Natural resource
   d. 130-30 fund

Chapter 12. EXTERNALITIES AND CONFLICTING RIGHTS

6. Many _____ are related to the environmental consequences of production and use

   - Systemic risk describes the risks to the overall economy arising from the risks which the banking system takes. That the private costs of banking failure may be smaller than the social costs justifies banking regulations, although regulations could create a moral hazard.

   - Anthropogenic climate change is attributed to greenhouse gas emissions from burning oil, gas, and coal. Global warming has been ranked as the #1 externality of all economic activity, in the magnitude of potential harms and yet remains unmitigated.

   a. Total Economic Value
   c. Negative externalities
   b. Green certificate
   d. White certificates

7. Examples of _____ include:

   - A beekeeper keeps the bees for their honey. A side effect or externality associated with his activity is the pollination of surrounding crops by the bees. The value generated by the pollination may be more important than the value of the harvested honey.

   - An individual planting an attractive garden in front of his house may provide benefits to others living in the area, and even financial benefits in the form of increased property values for all property owners.

   - An individual buying a product that is interconnected in a network (e.g., a video cellphone) will increase the usefulness of such phones to other people who have a video cellphone. When each new user of a product increases the value of the same product owned by others, the phenomenon is called a network externality or a network effect. Network externalities often have 'tipping points' where, suddenly, the product reaches general acceptance and near-universal usage, a phenomenon which can be seen in the near universal take-up of cellphones in some Scandinavian countries.

   - Knowledge spillover of inventions and information - once an invention (or most other forms of practical information) is discovered or made more easily accessible, others benefit by exploiting the invention or information. Copyright and intellectual property law are mechanisms to allow the inventor or creator to benefit from a temporary, state-protected monopoly in return for 'sharing' the information through publication or other means.

   a. Weighted average cost of carbon
   c. Negative externalities
   b. Total Economic Value
   d. Positive externalities

8. _____ in economics and business is the result of an exchange and from that trade we assign a numerical monetary value to a good, service or asset. If Alice trades Bob 4 apples for an orange, the _____ of an orange is 4 apples. Inversely, the _____ of an apple is 1/4 oranges.
   a. Price war
   c. Premium pricing
   b. Price book
   d. Price

9. A _____ is a normalized average (typically a weighted average) of prices for a given class of goods or services in a given region, during a given interval of time. It is a statistic designed to help to compare how these prices, taken as a whole, differ between time periods or geographical locations.

Price indices have several potential uses.

a. Transactional Net Margin Method
b. Product sabotage
c. Two-part tariff
d. Price Index

10. Necessary _____s:

If x is a necessary _____ of y, then the presence of y necessarily implies the presence of x. The presence of x, however, does not imply that y will occur.

Sufficient _____s:

If x is a sufficient _____ of y, then the presence of x necessarily implies the presence of y.

a. Materialism
b. Philosophy of economics
c. Political philosophy
d. Cause

11. An _____ is the magnum opus of the Scottish economist Adam Smith. It is a clearly written account of economics at the dawn of the Industrial Revolution, as well as a rhetorical piece written for the generally educated individual of the 18th century - advocating a free market economy as more productive and more beneficial to society.

The work is credited as a watershed in history and economics due to its comprehensive, largely accurate characterization of economic mechanisms that survive in modern economics; and also for its effective use of rhetorical technique, including structuring the work to contrast real world examples of free and fettered markets.

a. ACCRA Cost of Living Index
b. ACEA agreement
c. AD-IA Model
d. Inquiry into the Nature and Causes of the Wealth of Nations

12. An Inquiry into the Nature and Causes of the _____ is the magnum opus of the Scottish economist Adam Smith. It is a clearly written account of economics at the dawn of the Industrial Revolution, as well as a rhetorical piece written for the generally educated individual of the 18th century - advocating a free market economy as more productive and more beneficial to society.

The work is credited as a watershed in history and economics due to its comprehensive, largely accurate characterization of economic mechanisms that survive in modern economics; and also for its effective use of rhetorical technique, including structuring the work to contrast real world examples of free and fettered markets.

a. The Rise and Fall of the Great Powers
b. The Bell Curve
c. Black Book of Communism
d. Wealth of Nations

13. A _____ occurs when an entity spends more money than it takes in. The opposite of a _____ is a budget surplus. Debt is essentially an accumulated flow of deficits.

Chapter 12. EXTERNALITIES AND CONFLICTING RIGHTS

a. Public Financial Management
b. Budget deficit
c. Funding body
d. Lump-sum tax

14. An Inquiry into the Nature and Causes of _____ is the magnum opus of the Scottish economist Adam Smith. It is a clearly written account of economics at the dawn of the Industrial Revolution, as well as a rhetorical piece written for the generally educated individual of the 18th century - advocating a free market economy as more productive and more beneficial to society.

The work is credited as a watershed in history and economics due to its comprehensive, largely accurate characterization of economic mechanisms that survive in modern economics; and also for its effective use of rhetorical technique, including structuring the work to contrast real world examples of free and fettered markets.

a. The Rise and Fall of the Great Powers
b. The Wealth of Nations
c. Capital and Interest
d. Banks and Politics in America

15. In economics and related disciplines, a _____ is a cost incurred in making an economic exchange. For example, most people, when buying or selling a stock, must pay a commission to their broker; that commission is a _____ of doing the stock deal. Or consider buying a banana from a store; to purchase the banana, your costs will be not only the price of the banana itself, but also the energy and effort it requires to find out which of the various banana products you prefer, where to get them and at what price, the cost of traveling from your house to the store and back, the time waiting in line, and the effort of the paying itself; the costs above and beyond the cost of the banana are the _____s.

a. Transaction cost
b. Cost of poor quality
c. Sliding scale fees
d. Cost allocation

16. _____ is a fee paid on borrowed assets. It is the price paid for the use of borrowed money , or, money earned by deposited funds . Assets that are sometimes lent with _____ include money, shares, consumer goods through hire purchase, major assets such as aircraft, and even entire factories in finance lease arrangements.

a. Insolvency
b. Asset protection
c. Interest
d. Internal debt

17. In economics, the _____ is a historical inverse relation between the rate of unemployment and the rate of inflation in an economy. Stated simply, the lower the unemployment in an economy, the higher the rate of increase in nominal wages in the economy. Rate of Change of Wages against Unemployment, United Kingdom 1913-1948 from Phillips (1958)

William Phillips, a New Zealand born economist, wrote a paper in 1958 titled The Relationship between Unemployment and the Rate of Change of Money Wages in the United Kingdom 1861-1957, which was published in the quarterly journal Economica.

a. Cost curve
b. Lorenz curve
c. Demand curve
d. Phillips curve

18. _____s is the social science that studies the production, distribution, and consumption of goods and services. The term _____s comes from the Ancient Greek oá¼°κονομῖα from oá¼¶κος (oikos, 'house') + vÏŒμος (nomos, 'custom' or 'law'), hence 'rules of the house(hold)'. Current _____ models developed out of the broader field of political economy in the late 19th century, owing to a desire to use an empirical approach more akin to the physical sciences.

Chapter 12. EXTERNALITIES AND CONFLICTING RIGHTS

a. Inflation
b. Opportunity cost
c. Energy economics
d. Economic

19. _____ is a term used in economic research and policy debates. As with freedom generally, there are various definitions, but no universally accepted concept of _____. One major approach to _____ comes from the libertarian tradition emphasizing free markets and private property, while another extends the welfare economics study of individual choice, with greater _____ coming from a 'larger' (in some technical sense) set of possible choices.

a. Economic liberalization
b. International sanctions
c. Investment policy
d. Economic Freedom

20. In economics, _____ is the difference between a company's total revenue and its opportunity costs. It is the increase in wealth that an investor has from making an investment, taking into consideration all costs associated with that investment including the opportunity cost of capital.

Profit is the factor income of the entrepreneur.

a. Operating profit
b. Accounting profit
c. Economic profit
d. ACCRA Cost of Living Index

21. The accounting equation relates assets, _____, and owner's equity:

Assets = _____ + Owner's Equity

The accounting equation is the mathematical structure of the balance sheet.

The Australian Accounting Research Foundation defines _____ as: 'future sacrifice of economic benefits that the entity is presently obliged to make to other entities as a result of past transactions and other past events.'

Probably the most accepted accounting definition of liability is the one used by the International Accounting Standards Board (IASB.) The following is a quotation from IFRS Framework:

A liability is a present obligation of the enterprise arising from past events, the settlement of which is expected to result in an outflow from the enterprise of resources embodying economic benefits

-

Regulations as to the recognition of _____ are different all over the world, but are roughly similar to those of the IASB.

a. Liabilities
b. Coase theorem
c. Community property
d. Competition law theory

22. In economics and finance, _____ is the change in total cost that arises when the quantity produced changes by one unit. It is the cost of producing one more unit of a good. Mathematically, the _____ function is expressed as the first derivative of the total cost (TC) function with respect to quantity (Q.)

Chapter 12. EXTERNALITIES AND CONFLICTING RIGHTS

a. Variable cost
b. Marginal cost
c. Quality costs
d. Khozraschyot

23. The _____ of monetary management established the rules for commercial and financial relations among the world's major industrial states in the mid 20th Century. The _____ was the first example of a fully negotiated monetary order intended to govern monetary relations among independent nation-states.

Preparing to rebuild the international economic system as World War II was still raging, 730 delegates from all 44 Allied nations gathered at the Mount Washington Hotel in Bretton Woods, New Hampshire, United States, for the United Nations Monetary and Financial Conference.

a. 100-year flood
b. 1921 recession
c. 130-30 fund
d. Bretton Woods system

24. In economics, an _____ or spillover of an economic transaction is an impact on a party that is not directly involved in the transaction. In such a case, prices do not reflect the full costs or benefits in production or consumption of a product or service. A positive impact is called an external benefit, while a negative impact is called an external cost.

a. Environmental impact assessment
b. Environmental tariff
c. Externality
d. Existence value

25. _____ or congestion charges is a system of surcharging users of a transport network in periods of peak demand to reduce traffic congestion. Examples include some toll-like road pricing fees, and higher peak charges for utilities, public transport and slots in canals and airports. This variable pricing strategy regulates demand, making it possible to manage congestion without increasing supply.

a. 100-year flood
b. 1921 recession
c. Congestion pricing
d. 130-30 fund

26. _____ is one of the four Ps of the marketing mix. The other three aspects are product, promotion, and place. It is also a key variable in microeconomic price allocation theory.

a. Premium pricing
b. Pricing
c. Point of total assumption
d. Guaranteed Maximum Price

Chapter 13. MARKETS AND GOVERNMENT

1. _____ is that which is owed; usually referencing assets owed, but the term can also cover moral obligations and other interactions not requiring money. In the case of assets, _____ is a means of using future purchasing power in the present before a summation has been earned. Some companies and corporations use _____ as a part of their overall corporate finance strategy.

   a. Debt
   b. Hard money loan
   c. Collateral Management
   d. Debenture

2. A _____ occurs when an entity spends more money than it takes in. The opposite of a _____ is a budget surplus. Debt is essentially an accumulated flow of deficits.

   a. Funding body
   b. Public Financial Management
   c. Lump-sum tax
   d. Budget deficit

3. _____ is a fee paid on borrowed assets. It is the price paid for the use of borrowed money, or, money earned by deposited funds. Assets that are sometimes lent with _____ include money, shares, consumer goods through hire purchase, major assets such as aircraft, and even entire factories in finance lease arrangements.

   a. Interest
   b. Internal debt
   c. Asset protection
   d. Insolvency

4. In economics, a _____ exists when the production or use of goods and services by the market is not efficient. That is, there exists another outcome where all involved can be made better off. _____s can be viewed as scenarios where individuals' pursuit of pure self-interest leads to results that are not efficient - that can be improved upon from the societal point-of-view.

   a. Fixed exchange rate
   b. Financial economics
   c. General equilibrium
   d. Market failure

5. Examples of _____ include:

   - A beekeeper keeps the bees for their honey. A side effect or externality associated with his activity is the pollination of surrounding crops by the bees. The value generated by the pollination may be more important than the value of the harvested honey.

   - An individual planting an attractive garden in front of his house may provide benefits to others living in the area, and even financial benefits in the form of increased property values for all property owners.

   - An individual buying a product that is interconnected in a network (e.g., a video cellphone) will increase the usefulness of such phones to other people who have a video cellphone. When each new user of a product increases the value of the same product owned by others, the phenomenon is called a network externality or a network effect. Network externalities often have 'tipping points' where, suddenly, the product reaches general acceptance and near-universal usage, a phenomenon which can be seen in the near universal take-up of cellphones in some Scandinavian countries.

   - Knowledge spillover of inventions and information - once an invention (or most other forms of practical information) is discovered or made more easily accessible, others benefit by exploiting the invention or information. Copyright and intellectual property law are mechanisms to allow the inventor or creator to benefit from a temporary, state-protected monopoly in return for 'sharing' the information through publication or other means.

Chapter 13. MARKETS AND GOVERNMENT

a. Positive externalities
c. Negative externalities

b. Weighted average cost of carbon
d. Total Economic Value

6. In economics, the _____ is that part of the economy which is both run for private profit and is not controlled by the state. By contrast, enterprises that are part of the state are part of the public sector; private, non-profit organizations are regarded as part of the voluntary sector.

A variety of legal structures exist for _____ business organizations, depending on the jurisdiction in which they have their legal domicile.

a. Standard Industrial Classification
c. Secondary sector of the economy

b. Primary products
d. Private sector

7. The _____ is the part of economic and administrative life that deals with the delivery of goods and services by and for the government, whether national, regional or local/municipal.

Examples of _____ activity range from delivering social security, administering urban planning and organising national defenses.

The organization of the _____ can take several forms, including:

- Direct administration funded through taxation; the delivering organization generally has no specific requirement to meet commercial success criteria, and production decisions are determined by government.
- Publicly owned corporations (in some contexts, especially manufacturing, 'state-owned enterprises'); which differ from direct administration in that they have greater commercial freedoms and are expected to operate according to commercial criteria, and production decisions are not generally taken by government (although goals may be set for them by government.)
- Partial outsourcing (of the scale many businesses do, e.g. for IT services), is considered a _____ model.

A borderline form is

- Complete outsourcing or contracting out, with a privately owned corporation delivering the entire service on behalf of government. This may be considered a mixture of private sector operations with public ownership of assets, although in some forms the private sector's control and/or risk is so great that the service may no longer be considered part of the _____.

a. Public sector
c. 100-year flood

b. Policy cycle
d. 130-30 fund

8. _____s is the social science that studies the production, distribution, and consumption of goods and services. The term _____s comes from the Ancient Greek oá¼°κονομῖα from oá¼¶κος (oikos, 'house') + vÏŒμος (nomos, 'custom' or 'law'), hence 'rules of the house(hold)'. Current _____ models developed out of the broader field of political economy in the late 19th century, owing to a desire to use an empirical approach more akin to the physical sciences.

a. Opportunity cost
b. Energy economics
c. Inflation
d. Economic

9. _____ is a term used in economic research and policy debates. As with freedom generally, there are various definitions, but no universally accepted concept of _____. One major approach to _____ comes from the libertarian tradition emphasizing free markets and private property, while another extends the welfare economics study of individual choice, with greater _____ coming from a 'larger' (in some technical sense) set of possible choices.

a. Investment policy
b. International sanctions
c. Economic liberalization
d. Economic Freedom

Chapter 13. MARKETS AND GOVERNMENT

10. A _____ is:

- Rewrite _____, in generative grammar and computer science
- Standardization, a formal and widely-accepted statement, fact, definition, or qualification
- Operation, a determinate _____ for performing a mathematical operation and obtaining a certain result (Mathematics, Logic)
    - Unary operation
    - Binary operation
- _____ of inference, a function from sets of formulae to formulae (Mathematics, Logic)
- _____ of thumb, principle with broad application that is not intended to be strictly accurate or reliable for every situation. Also often simply referred to as a _____
- Moral, an atomic element of a moral code for guiding choices in human behavior
- Heuristic, a quantized '_____' which shows a tendency or probability for successful function
- A regulation, as in sports
- A Production _____, as in computer science
- Procedural law, a _____ set governing the application of laws to cases
    - A law, which may informally be called a '_____'
    - A court ruling, a decision by a court
- In the U.S. Government, a regulation mandated by Congress, but written or expanded upon by the Executive Branch.
- Norm (sociology), an informal but widely accepted _____, concept, truth, definition, or qualification (social norms, legal norms, coding norms)
- Norm (philosophy), a kind of sentence or a reason to act, feel or believe
- 'Rulership' is the concept of governance by a government:
    - Military _____, governance by a military body
    - Monastic _____, a collection of precepts that guides the life of monks or nuns in a religious order where the superior holds the place of Christ
- Slide _____

- '_____,' a song by Ayumi Hamasaki
- '_____,' a song by rapper Nas
- '_____s,' an album by the band The Whitest Boy Alive
- _____s: Pyaar Ka Superhit Formula, a 2003 Bollywood film
- ruler, an instrument for measuring lengths
- _____, a component of an astrolabe, circumferator or similar instrument
- The _____s, a bestselling self-help book
- _____ Project (Run Up-to-date Linux Everywhere), a project that aims to use up-to-date Linux software on old PCs
- _____ engine, a software system that helps managing business _____s
- Ja _____, a hip hop artist
    - R.U.L.E., a 2005 greatest hits album by rapper Ja _____
- '_____s,' a KMFDM song

a. Procter ' Gamble   b. Demand
c. Technocracy   d. Rule

Chapter 13. MARKETS AND GOVERNMENT

11. Economics:

    - _____,the desire to own something and the ability to pay for it
    - _____ curve,a graphic representation of a _____ schedule
    - _____ deposit, the money in checking accounts
    - _____ pull theory,the theory that inflation occurs when _____ for goods and services exceeds existing supplies
    - _____ schedule,a table that lists the quantity of a good a person will buy it each different price
    - _____ side economics,the school of economics at believes government spending and tax cuts open economy by raising _____

    a. Variability
    b. Production
    c. McKesson ' Robbins scandal
    d. Demand

12. In economics, the _____ can be defined as the graph depicting the relationship between the price of a certain commodity, and the amount of it that consumers are willing and able to purchase at that given price. It is a graphic representation of a demand schedule. The _____ for all consumers together follows from the _____ of every individual consumer: the individual demands at each price are added together.

    a. Wage curve
    b. Cost curve
    c. Kuznets curve
    d. Demand curve

13. In finance, the term _____ describes various legal measures taken to ensure that debtors, whether individuals, businesses honor their debts and make an honest effort to repay the money that they owe. Generally regarded as a subdivision of tax law, _____ is most often enforced through a combination of audits and legal restrictions. For example, a provision of the Federal Debt Collection Procedure Act states that a person or organization indebted to the United States, against whom a judgment lien has been filed, is ineligible to receive a government grant.

    a. Hard money loan
    b. Carryback loan
    c. Microcredit
    d. Debt compliance

14. A _____ is the exclusive authority to determine how a resource is used, whether that resource is owned by government or by individuals. All economic goods have a _____s attribute. This attribute has three broad components

    1. The right to use the good
    2. The right to earn income from the good
    3. The right to transfer the good to others

    The concept of _____s as used by economists and legal scholars are related but distinct. The distinction is largely seen in the economists' focus on the ability of an individual or collective to control the use of the good.

    a. Post-sale restraint
    b. Holder in due course
    c. High-reeve
    d. Property right

15. _____ was a survey conducted by the U.S. Department of Justice to gauge the prevalence of alcohol and illegal drug use among prior arrestees. It was a reformulation of the prior Drug Use Forecasting (DUF) program, focused on five drugs in particular: cocaine, marijuana, methamphetamine, opiates, and PCP.

Chapter 13. MARKETS AND GOVERNMENT

Participants were randomly selected from arrest records in major metropolitan areas; because no personally identifying information is taken from each record chosen, the resulting data can be correlated to arrest rates, but not to the total population of persons charged.

a. Arrestee Drug Abuse Monitoring
b. AD-IA Model
c. ACCRA Cost of Living Index
d. ACEA agreement

16. An _____ or Å"conomic system is a system that involves the production, distribution and consumption of goods and services between the entities in a particular society. It is the method used by society to produce and distribute goods and services. The _____ is composed of people and institutions, including their relationships to productive resources, such as through the convention of property.

a. Indicative planning
b. Information economy
c. Intention economy
d. Economic system

17. In economics and related disciplines, a _____ is a cost incurred in making an economic exchange. For example, most people, when buying or selling a stock, must pay a commission to their broker; that commission is a _____ of doing the stock deal. Or consider buying a banana from a store; to purchase the banana, your costs will be not only the price of the banana itself, but also the energy and effort it requires to find out which of the various banana products you prefer, where to get them and at what price, the cost of traveling from your house to the store and back, the time waiting in line, and the effort of the paying itself; the costs above and beyond the cost of the banana are the _____s.

a. Cost allocation
b. Sliding scale fees
c. Transaction cost
d. Cost of poor quality

18. The _____ is a US private, nonprofit research organization dedicated to studying the science and empirics of economics, especially the American economy. It is 'committed to undertaking and disseminating unbiased economic research among public policymakers, business professionals, and the academic community.' It publishes NBER Working Papers and books. The NBER is located in Cambridge, Massachusetts with branch offices in Palo Alto, California, and New York City.

a. Deutsche Bank
b. CEFTA
c. Non-governmental organization
d. National Bureau of Economic Research

19. In economics, _____ is the transfer of income, wealth or property from some individuals to others.

One premise of _____ is that money should be distributed to benefit the poorer members of society, and that the rich have an obligation to assist the poor, thus creating a more financially egalitarian society. Another argument is that the rich exploit the poor or otherwise gain unfair benefits.

a. 100-year flood
b. 130-30 fund
c. 1921 recession
d. Redistribution

20. Child Protective Services (CPS) is the name of a governmental agency in many states of the United States that responds to reports of child abuse or neglect. Some states use other names, often attempting to reflect more family-centered (as opposed to child-centered) practices, such as 'Department of Children ' Family Services' (DCFS.) CPS is also known by the name of 'Department of _____s' (Dsocial service) or simply '_____s.'

Chapter 13. MARKETS AND GOVERNMENT

CPS agencies operate under authority assigned to them by the individual state legislatures, and generally perform a series of functions that can be identified as follows:

1. Intake: Receive reports of child maltreatment allegations. In most states, mostly everyone is a mandatory reporter, especially public safety personnel (fire, police, etc.), public _____ workers, school staff, day care staff, and more. One exception is attorneys representing clients on child-maltreatment criminal charges; and, substance-abuse treatment providers.
2. Screening the Report: Determine if a report's allegations meet statutory definitions for child maltreatment. If statutory definitions (State law) are met, then the report is accepted for investigation/assessment and a case is opened; otherwise, it is screened out, and might be forwarded to another agency for follow up supportive services to prevent child maltreatment.
3. Investigation/Assessment: To determine if a received report on an open case is substantiated to be true, then CPS social workers, as agents of the Juvenile Court, 'investigate' or 'assess' the allegations through contacts with the family and pertinent collateral-information providers (school staff, neighbors, etc.). Home visits are usually included although different states have different restrictions regarding this. After completion of the investigation, if the allegations are substantiated, a report is made to the Juvenile Court with a petition for action and recommendations for disposition. If the allegations are unsubstantiated (found not true), the case is closed.
4. Case Decision and Disposition: If the child-maltreatment allegations prove sufficiently credible (substantiated), a petition is filed with the Juvenile Court to take action. This petition may be to remove the child from the custody of the parents or legal guardian. If the petition is approved by the Juvenile Court, the Court makes findings of jurisdiction and disposition. The child is then considered to be adjudicated as a ward of the Court, and placed under the custody and care of the CPS agency, supervised by the Court. The child remains under the custody of the Court until proof is provided that the child can safely return to the care and custody of the parents or guardian from which they were removed.(.

a. Social service
b. 130-30 fund
c. 100-year flood
d. 1921 recession

21. In economics, the _____ is a historical inverse relation between the rate of unemployment and the rate of inflation in an economy. Stated simply, the lower the unemployment in an economy, the higher the rate of increase in nominal wages in the economy. Rate of Change of Wages against Unemployment, United Kingdom 1913-1948 from Phillips (1958)

William Phillips, a New Zealand born economist, wrote a paper in 1958 titled The Relationship between Unemployment and the Rate of Change of Money Wages in the United Kingdom 1861-1957, which was published in the quarterly journal Economica.

a. Demand curve
b. Phillips curve
c. Cost curve
d. Lorenz curve

22. The _____ refers to the 'common well-being' or 'general welfare.' The _____ is central to policy debates, politics, democracy and the nature of government itself. While nearly everyone claims that aiding the common well-being or general welfare is positive, there is little, if any, consensus on what exactly constitutes the _____.

Chapter 13. MARKETS AND GOVERNMENT

There are different views on how many members of the public must benefit from an action before it can be declared to be in the _____: at one extreme, an action has to benefit every single member of society in order to be truly in the _____; at the other extreme, any action can be in the _____ as long as it benefits some of the population and harms none.

- a. Stealth tax
- b. Second-class citizen
- c. Power Elite
- d. Public interest

23. The accounting equation relates assets, _____, and owner's equity:

   Assets = _____ + Owner's Equity

The accounting equation is the mathematical structure of the balance sheet.

The Australian Accounting Research Foundation defines _____ as: 'future sacrifice of economic benefits that the entity is presently obliged to make to other entities as a result of past transactions and other past events.'

Probably the most accepted accounting definition of liability is the one used by the International Accounting Standards Board (IASB.) The following is a quotation from IFRS Framework:

A liability is a present obligation of the enterprise arising from past events, the settlement of which is expected to result in an outflow from the enterprise of resources embodying economic benefits

-

Regulations as to the recognition of _____ are different all over the world, but are roughly similar to those of the IASB.

- a. Coase theorem
- b. Competition law theory
- c. Community property
- d. Liabilities

24. _____ is the practice of influencing decisions made by government. It includes all attempts to influence legislators and officials, whether by other legislators, constituents or organized groups. A lobbyist is a person who tries to influence legislation on behalf of a special interest or a member of a lobby.
- a. Adam Smith
- b. Lobbying
- c. Adolf Hitler
- d. Adolph Fischer

25. _____ originally was the term for studying production, buying and selling, and their relations with law, custom, and government. _____ originated in moral philosophy. It developed in the 18th century as the study of the economies of states -- polities, hence _____.
- a. Political Economy
- b. Productive and unproductive labour
- c. Dirigisme
- d. Geoeconomics

26. _____ by John Stuart Mill was the most important economics or political economy textbook of the mid nineteenth century. It was revised until its seventh edition in 1871, shortly before Mill's death in 1873, and republished in numerous other editions.

Mill's Principles were written in a style of prose far flung from the introductory texts of today.

   a. Principles of Political Economy
   b. Limits to Growth
   c. Principles of Political Economy and Taxation
   d. The Rise and Fall of the Great Powers

27. On the _____ is a book by David Ricardo on economics. The book concludes that land rent grows as population increases. It also clearly lays out the theory of comparative advantage, which shows that all nations can benefit from free trade, even if a nation lacks an absolute advantage in all sectors of its economy.

   a. Butterfly Economics
   b. The Wealth of Nations
   c. Principles of Political Economy and Taxation
   d. Theory of Moral Sentiments

Chapter 14. THE OVERALL PERFORMANCE OF ECONOMIC SYSTEMS

1. _____s is the social science that studies the production, distribution, and consumption of goods and services. The term _____s comes from the Ancient Greek oá¼°κονομῖα from oá¼¶κος (oikos, 'house') + vĭŒμος (nomos, 'custom' or 'law'), hence 'rules of the house(hold)'. Current _____ models developed out of the broader field of political economy in the late 19th century, owing to a desire to use an empirical approach more akin to the physical sciences.

   a. Inflation
   b. Energy economics
   c. Opportunity cost
   d. Economic

2. _____ is a term used in economic research and policy debates. As with freedom generally, there are various definitions, but no universally accepted concept of _____. One major approach to _____ comes from the libertarian tradition emphasizing free markets and private property, while another extends the welfare economics study of individual choice, with greater _____ coming from a 'larger' (in some technical sense) set of possible choices.

   a. Investment policy
   b. International sanctions
   c. Economic liberalization
   d. Economic Freedom

3. The _____ or gross domestic income (GDI), a basic measure of an economy's economic performance, is the market value of all final goods and services produced within the borders of a nation in a year. _____ can be defined in three ways, all of which are conceptually identical. First, it is equal to the total expenditures for all final goods and services produced within the country in a stipulated period of time (usually a 365-day year.)

   a. Market structure
   b. Monopolistic competition
   c. Countercyclical
   d. Gross domestic product

4. _____ was a survey conducted by the U.S. Department of Justice to gauge the prevalence of alcohol and illegal drug use among prior arrestees. It was a reformulation of the prior Drug Use Forecasting (DUF) program, focused on five drugs in particular: cocaine, marijuana, methamphetamine, opiates, and PCP.

Participants were randomly selected from arrest records in major metropolitan areas; because no personally identifying information is taken from each record chosen, the resulting data can be correlated to arrest rates, but not to the total population of persons charged.

   a. ACCRA Cost of Living Index
   b. ACEA agreement
   c. AD-IA Model
   d. Arrestee Drug Abuse Monitoring

5. Necessary _____s:

If x is a necessary _____ of y, then the presence of y necessarily implies the presence of x. The presence of x, however, does not imply that y will occur.

Sufficient _____s:

If x is a sufficient _____ of y, then the presence of x necessarily implies the presence of y.

   a. Materialism
   b. Cause
   c. Political philosophy
   d. Philosophy of economics

6. The _____ consists of a number of economic theories which describe the nature of the firm, company including its existence, its behaviour, and its relationship with the market.

Chapter 14. THE OVERALL PERFORMANCE OF ECONOMIC SYSTEMS

In simplified terms, the _____ aims to answer these questions:

1. Existence - why do firms emerge, why are not all transactions in the economy mediated over the market?
2. Boundaries - why the boundary between firms and the market is located exactly there? Which transactions are performed internally and which are negotiated on the market?
3. Organization - why are firms structured in such specific way? What is the interplay of formal and informal relationships?

Despite looking simple, these questions are not answered by the established economic theory, which usually views firms as given, and treats them as black boxes without any internal structure.

The First World War period saw a change of emphasis in economic theory away from industry-level analysis which mainly included analysing markets to analysis at the level of the firm, as it became increasingly clear that perfect competition was no longer an adequate model of how firms behaved. Economic theory till then had focussed on trying to understand markets alone and there had been little study on understanding why firms or organisations exist.

a. Policy Ineffectiveness Proposition
b. Theory of the firm
c. Technology gap
d. Khazzoom-Brookes postulate

7. An _____ is the magnum opus of the Scottish economist Adam Smith. It is a clearly written account of economics at the dawn of the Industrial Revolution, as well as a rhetorical piece written for the generally educated individual of the 18th century - advocating a free market economy as more productive and more beneficial to society.

The work is credited as a watershed in history and economics due to its comprehensive, largely accurate characterization of economic mechanisms that survive in modern economics; and also for its effective use of rhetorical technique, including structuring the work to contrast real world examples of free and fettered markets.

a. ACCRA Cost of Living Index
b. ACEA agreement
c. AD-IA Model
d. Inquiry into the Nature and Causes of the Wealth of Nations

8. An Inquiry into the Nature and Causes of the _____ is the magnum opus of the Scottish economist Adam Smith. It is a clearly written account of economics at the dawn of the Industrial Revolution, as well as a rhetorical piece written for the generally educated individual of the 18th century - advocating a free market economy as more productive and more beneficial to society.

The work is credited as a watershed in history and economics due to its comprehensive, largely accurate characterization of economic mechanisms that survive in modern economics; and also for its effective use of rhetorical technique, including structuring the work to contrast real world examples of free and fettered markets.

a. Wealth of Nations
b. The Rise and Fall of the Great Powers
c. Black Book of Communism
d. The Bell Curve

Chapter 14. THE OVERALL PERFORMANCE OF ECONOMIC SYSTEMS

9. A _____ occurs when an entity spends more money than it takes in. The opposite of a _____ is a budget surplus. Debt is essentially an accumulated flow of deficits.
   a. Funding body
   b. Lump-sum tax
   c. Public Financial Management
   d. Budget deficit

10. In economics _____s are goods that are ultimately consumed rather than used in the production of another good. For example, a car sold to a consumer is a _____; the components such as tires sold to the car manufacturer are not; they are intermediate goods used to make the _____.

    When used in measures of national income and output the term _____s only includes new goods.

   a. Substitute good
   b. Luxury good
   c. Goods and services
   d. Final good

11. A _____ is an object whose consumption increases the utility of the consumer, for which the quantity demanded exceeds the quantity supplied at zero price. _____s are usually modeled as having diminishing marginal utility. The first individual purchase has high utility; the second has less.
   a. Merit good
   b. Good
   c. Pie method
   d. Composite good

12. _____ or producer goods are goods used as inputs in the production of other goods, such as partly finished goods. They are goods used in production of final goods. A firm may make then use _____, or make then sell, or buy then use them.
   a. Intermediate goods
   b. Income distribution
   c. Inflation adjustment
   d. Economic forecasting

13. _____ is the price at which an asset would trade in a competitive Walrasian auction setting. _____ is often used interchangeably with open _____, fair value or fair _____, although these terms have distinct definitions in different standards, and may differ in some circumstances.

    International Valuation Standards defines _____ as 'the estimated amount for which a property should exchange on the date of valuation between a willing buyer and a willing seller in an arm's-length transaction after proper marketing wherein the parties had each acted knowledgeably, prudently, and without compulsion.'

    _____ is a concept distinct from market price, which is 'the price at which one can transact', while _____ is 'the true underlying value' according to theoretical standards.

   a. Secured loan
   b. Netting
   c. Personal financial management
   d. Market value

14. An Inquiry into the Nature and Causes of _____ is the magnum opus of the Scottish economist Adam Smith. It is a clearly written account of economics at the dawn of the Industrial Revolution, as well as a rhetorical piece written for the generally educated individual of the 18th century - advocating a free market economy as more productive and more beneficial to society.

Chapter 14. THE OVERALL PERFORMANCE OF ECONOMIC SYSTEMS

The work is credited as a watershed in history and economics due to its comprehensive, largely accurate characterization of economic mechanisms that survive in modern economics; and also for its effective use of rhetorical technique, including structuring the work to contrast real world examples of free and fettered markets.

a. Banks and Politics in America
b. The Rise and Fall of the Great Powers
c. Capital and Interest
d. The Wealth of Nations

15. _____ is the a method of technical and economic research of the systems for purpose to optimize a parity between system's consumer functions or properties and expenses to achieve those functions or properties.

This methodology for continuous perfection of production, industrial technologies, organizational structures was developed by Juryj Sobolev in 1948 at the 'Perm telephone factory'

- 1948 Juryj Sobolev - the first success in application of a method analysis at the 'Perm telephone factory'.
- 1949 - the first application for the invention as result of use of the new method.

Today in economically developed countries practically each enterprise or the company use methodology of the kind of functional-cost analysis as a practice of the quality management, most full satisfying to principles of standards of series ISO 9000.

- Interest of consumer not in products itself, but the advantage which it will receive from its usage.
- The consumer aspires to reduce his expenses
- Functions needed by consumer can be executed in the various ways, and, hence, with various efficiency and expenses. Among possible alternatives of realization of functions exist such in which the parity of quality and the price is the optimal for the consumer.

The goal of _____ is achievement of the highest consumer satisfaction of production at simultaneous decrease in all kinds of industrial expenses Classical _____ has three English synonyms - Value Engineering, Value Management, Value Analysis.

a. Monopoly wage
b. Staple financing
c. Willingness to pay
d. Function cost analysis

16. A variety of measures of national income and output are used in economics to estimate total economic activity in a country or region, including gross domestic product (GDP), _____ , and net national income (NNI.)

There are three main ways of calculating these numbers; the output approach, the income approach and the expenditure approach. In theory, the three must yield the same, because total expenditures on goods and services must equal the total income paid to the producers (GNI), and that must also equal the total value of the output of goods and services (_____.)

a. Purchasing power parity
b. Household final consumption expenditure
c. Gross world product
d. Gross national product

Chapter 14. THE OVERALL PERFORMANCE OF ECONOMIC SYSTEMS

17. The _____ is a US private, nonprofit research organization dedicated to studying the science and empirics of economics, especially the American economy. It is 'committed to undertaking and disseminating unbiased economic research among public policymakers, business professionals, and the academic community.' It publishes NBER Working Papers and books. The NBER is located in Cambridge, Massachusetts with branch offices in Palo Alto, California, and New York City.
   a. CEFTA
   b. Non-governmental organization
   c. Deutsche Bank
   d. National Bureau of Economic Research

18. _____ is the difference between price and the costs of bringing to market whatever it is that is accounted as an enterprise (whether by harvest, extraction, manufacture, or purchase) in terms of the component costs of delivered goods and/or services and any operating or other expenses.

A key difficulty in measuring profit is in defining costs. Pure economic monetary profits can be zero or negative even in competitive equilibrium when accounted monetized costs exceed monetized price.

   a. Economic profit
   b. ACCRA Cost of Living Index
   c. Operating profit
   d. Accounting profit

19. _____ is a fee paid on borrowed assets. It is the price paid for the use of borrowed money , or, money earned by deposited funds . Assets that are sometimes lent with _____ include money, shares, consumer goods through hire purchase, major assets such as aircraft, and even entire factories in finance lease arrangements.
   a. Interest
   b. Asset protection
   c. Insolvency
   d. Internal debt

20. A variety of measures of _____ and output are used in economics to estimate total economic activity in a country or region, including gross domestic product (GDP), gross national product (GNP), and net _____

There are three main ways of calculating these numbers; the output approach, the income approach and the expenditure approach. In theory, the three must yield the same, because total expenditures on goods and services must equal the total income paid to the producers (Gnational income), and that must also equal the total value of the output of goods and services (GNP.)

   a. Gross world product
   b. GNI per capita
   c. Volume index
   d. National income

21. _____ refers to the additional value of a commodity over the cost of commodities used to produce it from the previous stage of production. An example is the price of gasoline at the pump over the price of the oil in it. In national accounts used in macroeconomics, it refers to the contribution of the factors of production, i.e., land, labor, and capital goods, to raising the value of a product and corresponds to the incomes received by the owners of these factors.
   a. Solow residual
   b. Full employment
   c. Hodrick-Prescott filter
   d. Value added

22. _____ is sometimes referred to as _____, actually it means Economic Monetary Union.

Chapter 14. THE OVERALL PERFORMANCE OF ECONOMIC SYSTEMS

First ideas of an economic and monetary union in Europe were raised well before establishing the European Communities. For example, already in the League of Nations, Gustav Stresemann asked in 1929 for a European currency (Link) against the background of an increased economic division due to a number of new nation states in Europe after WWI.

a. European Monetary System
b. Euro Interbank Offered Rate
c. Exchange rate mechanism
d. European Monetary Union

23. An economic and _____ is a single market with a common currency. It is to be distinguished from a mere currency union, which does not involve a single market. This is the fifth stage of economic integration.

a. Free trade zone
b. Monetary Union
c. Customs union
d. Commercial invoice

24. In economics, _____ is the difference between a company's total revenue and its opportunity costs. It is the increase in wealth that an investor has from making an investment, taking into consideration all costs associated with that investment including the opportunity cost of capital.

Profit is the factor income of the entrepreneur.

a. Operating profit
b. Accounting profit
c. ACCRA Cost of Living Index
d. Economic profit

25. The _____ was a regulatory body in the United States created by the Interstate Commerce Act of 1887, which was signed into law by President Grover Cleveland. The agency was abolished in 1995, and the agency's remaining functions were transferred to the Surface Transportation Board.

The Commission's five members were appointed by the President with the consent of the United States Senate.

a. ACCRA Cost of Living Index
b. Office of Thrift Supervision
c. ACEA agreement
d. Interstate Commerce Commission

26. _____ relates to the composition of GDP. What is produced in a certain country is naturally also sold, but some of the goods produced in a given year may not be sold the same year, but in later years. Conversely, some of the goods sold in a given year might have been produced in an earlier year.

a. Investment theory
b. Inventory investment
c. Obelisk International
d. Investment decisions

27. The _____ was a worldwide economic downturn starting in most places in 1929 and ending at different times in the 1930s or early 1940s for different countries. It was the largest and most important economic depression in the 20th century, and is used in the 21st century as an example of how far the world's economy can fall. The _____ originated in the United States; historians most often use as a starting date the stock market crash on October 29, 1929, known as Black Tuesday.

a. British Empire Economic Conference
b. Jarrow March
c. Great Depression
d. Wall Street Crash of 1929

Chapter 14. THE OVERALL PERFORMANCE OF ECONOMIC SYSTEMS

28. In economics, _____ is a sustained decrease in the general price level of goods and services. _____ occurs when the annual inflation rate falls below zero percent, resulting in an increase in the real value of money -- a negative inflation rate. This should not be confused with disinflation, a slow-down in the inflation rate (i.e. when the inflation decreases, but still remains positive.)
   a. Tobit model
   b. Literacy rate
   c. Price revolution
   d. Deflation

29. In statistics, a _____ is a value that allows data to be measured over time in terms of some base period ussually through a price index in order to distinguish between changes in the money value of GNP which result from a change in prices and those which result from a change in physical output. It is the measure of the price level for some quantity. A _____ serves as a price index in which the effects of inflation are nulled.
   a. Deflator
   b. Market microstructure
   c. Contingent employment
   d. Blanket order

30. In economics, _____ is a rise in the general level of prices of goods and services in an economy over a period of time. When the general price level rises, each unit of currency buys fewer goods and services; consequently, _____ is also a decline in the real value of money--a loss of purchasing power in the medium of exchange which is also the monetary unit of account in the economy. A chief measure of general price-level _____ is the general _____ rate, which is the percentage change in a general price index (normally the Consumer Price Index) over time.
   a. Economic
   b. Opportunity cost
   c. Inflation
   d. Energy economics

31. _____ is a macroeconomic measure of the size of an economy adjusted for price changes and inflation. It measures in constant prices the output of final goods and services and incomes within an economy. The formula for its definition is [(Nominal GDP)/(GDP deflator)] x 100, however, it is not calculated in this way.
   a. TED spread
   b. Real gross domestic product
   c. Bureau of Labor Statistics
   d. Gross world product

32. _____ is a broad label that refers to any individuals or households that use goods and services generated within the economy. The concept of a _____ is used in different contexts, so that the usage and significance of the term may vary.

Typically when business people and economists talk of _____s they are talking about person as _____, an aggregated commodity item with little individuality other than that expressed in the buy/not-buy decision.

   a. 130-30 fund
   b. 100-year flood
   c. 1921 recession
   d. Consumer

33. A _____ is a measure of the average price of consumer goods and services purchased by households. A _____ measures a price change for a constant market basket of goods and services from one period to the next within the same area (city, region, or nation.) It is a price index determined by measuring the price of a standard group of goods meant to represent the typical market basket of a typical urban consumer.
   a. Consumer Price Index
   b. Cost-of-living index
   c. Lipstick index
   d. CPI

Chapter 14. THE OVERALL PERFORMANCE OF ECONOMIC SYSTEMS

34. _____ in economics and business is the result of an exchange and from that trade we assign a numerical monetary value to a good, service or asset. If Alice trades Bob 4 apples for an orange, the _____ of an orange is 4 apples. Inversely, the _____ of an apple is 1/4 oranges.
   a. Premium pricing
   b. Price war
   c. Price book
   d. Price

35. A _____ is a normalized average (typically a weighted average) of prices for a given class of goods or services in a given region, during a given interval of time. It is a statistic designed to help to compare how these prices, taken as a whole, differ between time periods or geographical locations.

Price indices have several potential uses.

   a. Price Index
   b. Transactional Net Margin Method
   c. Product sabotage
   d. Two-part tariff

36. _____ is a decrease in the rate of inflation. This phase of the business cycle, in which retailers can no longer pass on higher prices to their customers, often occurs during a recession. In contrast, deflation occurs when prices are actually dropping.
   a. Disinflation
   b. Stealth inflation
   c. Mundell-Tobin effect
   d. Reflation

37. In finance, the term _____ describes various legal measures taken to ensure that debtors, whether individuals, businesses honor their debts and make an honest effort to repay the money that they owe. Generally regarded as a subdivision of tax law, _____ is most often enforced through a combination of audits and legal restrictions. For example, a provision of the Federal Debt Collection Procedure Act states that a person or organization indebted to the United States, against whom a judgment lien has been filed, is ineligible to receive a government grant.
   a. Carryback loan
   b. Debt compliance
   c. Hard money loan
   d. Microcredit

38. In economics, the _____ is a historical inverse relation between the rate of unemployment and the rate of inflation in an economy. Stated simply, the lower the unemployment in an economy, the higher the rate of increase in nominal wages in the economy. Rate of Change of Wages against Unemployment, United Kingdom 1913-1948 from Phillips (1958)

William Phillips, a New Zealand born economist, wrote a paper in 1958 titled The Relationship between Unemployment and the Rate of Change of Money Wages in the United Kingdom 1861-1957, which was published in the quarterly journal Economica.

   a. Lorenz curve
   b. Phillips curve
   c. Cost curve
   d. Demand curve

39. _____ is an economic situation in which inflation and economic stagnation occur simultaneously and remain unchecked for a period of time. The portmanteau _____ is generally attributed to British politician Iain Macleod, who coined the term in a speech to Parliament in 1965. The concept is notable partly because, in postwar macroeconomic theory, inflation and recession were regarded as mutually exclusive, and also because _____ has generally proven to be difficult and costly to eradicate once it gets started.

Chapter 14. THE OVERALL PERFORMANCE OF ECONOMIC SYSTEMS

a. Chronic inflation
c. Real interest rate
b. Stagflation
d. Price/wage spiral

40. The _____ is a theorem in probability that describes the long-term stability of the mean of a random variable. Given a random variable with a finite expected value, if its values are repeatedly sampled, as the number of these observations increases, the sample mean will tend to approach and stay close to the expected value (the average for the population.)

The LLN can easily be illustrated using the rolls of a die.

a. 130-30 fund
c. 100-year flood
b. 1921 recession
d. Law of large numbers

41. _____ was a Scottish moral philosopher and a pioneer of political economy. One of the key figures of the Scottish Enlightenment, Smith is the author of The Theory of Moral Sentiments and An Inquiry into the Nature and Causes of the Wealth of Nations. The latter, usually abbreviated as The Wealth of Nations, is considered his magnum opus and the first modern work of economics.

a. Adam Smith
c. Adolph Fischer
b. Alan Greenspan
d. Adolf Hitler

42. The underground economy or _____ is a market where all commerce is conducted without regard to taxation, law or regulations of trade. The term is also often known as the underdog, shadow economy, black economy, parallel economy or phantom trades.

In modern societies the underground economy covers a vast array of activities.

a. Market economy
c. Protectionism
b. Social market economy
d. Black market

43. In corporate finance, _____ is an estimate of true economic profit after making corrective adjustments to GAAP accounting, including deducting the opportunity cost of equity capital. _____ can be measured as Net Operating Profit After Taxes(or NOPAT) less the money cost of capital. _____ is similar in nature to that of calculating another financial performance measure - Residual Income , however, there are a few complexities involved with coming up with the elements for calculating _____ over RI such as the myriad adjustments that might be made to NOPAT before it is suitable for the formula below.

a. AD-IA Model
c. ACEA agreement
b. ACCRA Cost of Living Index
d. Economic value added

44. _____ is a branch of economics that studies how individuals, households and firms and some states make decisions to allocate limited resources, typically in markets where goods or services are being bought and sold. _____ examines how these decisions and behaviours affect the supply and demand for goods and services, which determines prices; and how prices, in turn , determine the supply and demand of goods and services.

Whereas macroeconomics involves the 'sum total of economic activity, dealing with the issues of growth, inflation and unemployment, and with national economic policies relating to these issues' and the effects of government actions on them.

a. Microeconomics
b. Recession
c. Countercyclical
d. New Keynesian economics

Chapter 15. EMPLOYMENT AND UNEMPLOYMENT

1. In economics, the _____ is a historical inverse relation between the rate of unemployment and the rate of inflation in an economy. Stated simply, the lower the unemployment in an economy, the higher the rate of increase in nominal wages in the economy. Rate of Change of Wages against Unemployment, United Kingdom 1913-1948 from Phillips (1958)

William Phillips, a New Zealand born economist, wrote a paper in 1958 titled The Relationship between Unemployment and the Rate of Change of Money Wages in the United Kingdom 1861-1957, which was published in the quarterly journal Economica.

   a. Phillips curve
   c. Demand curve
   b. Lorenz curve
   d. Cost curve

2. _____s is the social science that studies the production, distribution, and consumption of goods and services. The term _____s comes from the Ancient Greek οἰκονομῐ́α from οἶκος (oikos, 'house') + νόμος (nomos, 'custom' or 'law'), hence 'rules of the house(hold)'. Current _____ models developed out of the broader field of political economy in the late 19th century, owing to a desire to use an empirical approach more akin to the physical sciences.
   a. Energy economics
   c. Opportunity cost
   b. Inflation
   d. Economic

3. An _____ or Ä"conomic system is a system that involves the production, distribution and consumption of goods and services between the entities in a particular society. It is the method used by society to produce and distribute goods and services. The _____ is composed of people and institutions, including their relationships to productive resources, such as through the convention of property.
   a. Indicative planning
   c. Information economy
   b. Intention economy
   d. Economic system

4. _____ is a fee paid on borrowed assets. It is the price paid for the use of borrowed money, or, money earned by deposited funds. Assets that are sometimes lent with _____ include money, shares, consumer goods through hire purchase, major assets such as aircraft, and even entire factories in finance lease arrangements.
   a. Insolvency
   c. Asset protection
   b. Interest
   d. Internal debt

5. Economists distinguish between various types of unemployment, including cyclical unemployment, _____, structural unemployment and classical unemployment. Some additional types of unemployment that are occasionally mentioned are seasonal unemployment, hardcore unemployment, and hidden unemployment. Real-world unemployment may combine different types.
   a. Seasonal unemployment
   c. Frictional unemployment
   b. Types of unemployment
   d. Structural unemployment

6. Unemployment occurs when a person is available to work and seeking work but currently without work. The prevalence of unemployment is usually measured using the _____, which is defined as the percentage of those in the labor force who are unemployed. The _____ is also used in economic studies and economic indexes such as the United States' Conference Board's Index of Leading Indicators as a measure of the state of the macroeconomics.
   a. ACEA agreement
   c. AD-IA Model
   b. ACCRA Cost of Living Index
   d. Unemployment rate

Chapter 15. EMPLOYMENT AND UNEMPLOYMENT

7. _____ is a term used in economic research and policy debates. As with freedom generally, there are various definitions, but no universally accepted concept of _____. One major approach to _____ comes from the libertarian tradition emphasizing free markets and private property, while another extends the welfare economics study of individual choice, with greater _____ coming from a 'larger' (in some technical sense) set of possible choices.
   - a. Economic Freedom
   - b. International sanctions
   - c. Investment policy
   - d. Economic liberalization

8. In economics, the people in the _____ are the suppliers of labor. The _____ is all the nonmilitary people who are employed or unemployed. In 2005, the worldwide _____ was over 3 billion people.
   - a. Labor force
   - b. Distributed workforce
   - c. Departmentalization
   - d. Grenelle agreements

9. The accounting equation relates assets, _____, and owner's equity:

   Assets = _____ + Owner's Equity

The accounting equation is the mathematical structure of the balance sheet.

The Australian Accounting Research Foundation defines _____ as: 'future sacrifice of economic benefits that the entity is presently obliged to make to other entities as a result of past transactions and other past events.'

Probably the most accepted accounting definition of liability is the one used by the International Accounting Standards Board (IASB.) The following is a quotation from IFRS Framework:

A liability is a present obligation of the enterprise arising from past events, the settlement of which is expected to result in an outflow from the enterprise of resources embodying economic benefits

-

Regulations as to the recognition of _____ are different all over the world, but are roughly similar to those of the IASB.

   - a. Competition law theory
   - b. Coase theorem
   - c. Community property
   - d. Liabilities

10. The _____s were a social movement of British textile artisans in the early nineteenth century who protested--often by destroying mechanized looms--against the changes produced by the Industrial Revolution, which they felt were leaving them without work.

This English historical movement has to be seen in its context of the harsh economic climate due to the Napoleonic Wars, and the degrading working conditions in the new textile factories; but since then, the term _____ has been used derisively to describe anyone opposed to technological progress and technological change.

Chapter 15. EMPLOYMENT AND UNEMPLOYMENT

The _____ movement, which began in 1811 and 1812 when mills and pieces of factory machinery were burned by handloom weavers, took its name from the fictive Ned Ludd.

a. 100-year flood
b. 130-30 fund
c. 1921 recession
d. Luddite

11. The _____ is a US private, nonprofit research organization dedicated to studying the science and empirics of economics, especially the American economy. It is 'committed to undertaking and disseminating unbiased economic research among public policymakers, business professionals, and the academic community.' It publishes NBER Working Papers and books. The NBER is located in Cambridge, Massachusetts with branch offices in Palo Alto, California, and New York City.

a. CEFTA
b. Non-governmental organization
c. National Bureau of Economic Research
d. Deutsche Bank

12. The _____ is a concept of economic activity developed in particular by Milton Friedman and Edmund Phelps in the 1960s, both recipients of the Nobel prize in economics. In both cases, the development of the concept is cited as a main motivation behind the prize. It represents the hypothetical unemployment rate consistent with aggregate production being at the 'long-run' level.

a. Romer Model
b. Robertson lag
c. Real Business Cycle Theory
d. Natural rate of unemployment

13. In economics, a _____ is a general slowdown in economic activity over a sustained period of time, or a business cycle contraction. During _____s, many macroeconomic indicators vary in a similar way. Production as measured by Gross Domestic Product (GDP), employment, investment spending, capacity utilization, household incomes and business profits all fall during _____s.

a. Leading indicators
b. Treasury View
c. Monetary economics
d. Recession

14. Economics:

- _____, the desire to own something and the ability to pay for it
- _____ curve, a graphic representation of a _____ schedule
- _____ deposit, the money in checking accounts
- _____ pull theory, the theory that inflation occurs when _____ for goods and services exceeds existing supplies
- _____ schedule, a table that lists the quantity of a good a person will buy it each different price
- _____ side economics, the school of economics at believes government spending and tax cuts open economy by raising _____

a. Variability
b. Production
c. McKesson ' Robbins scandal
d. Demand

Chapter 15. EMPLOYMENT AND UNEMPLOYMENT

15. In labor economics, the _____ hypothesis argues that wages, at least in some markets, are determined by more than simply supply and demand. Specifically, it points to the incentive for managers to pay their employees more than the market-clearing wage in order to increase their productivity or efficiency. This increased labor productivity pays for the relatively higher wages.

   a. Exogenous growth model
   b. Earnings calls
   c. Inflatable rats
   d. Efficiency wage

16. _____ describes a deliberate attempt to interfere with the free and fair operation of the market and create artificial, false or misleading appearances with respect to the price of a security, commodity or currency. _____ is prohibited under Section 9(a)(2) of the Securities Exchange Act of 1934, and in Australia under Section s 1041A of the Corporations Act 2001. The Act defines _____ as transactions which create an artificial price or maintain an artificial price for a tradable security.

   a. Legal monopoly
   b. Net domestic product
   c. Managerial economics
   d. Market manipulation

17. _____ is an economic model based on price, utility and quantity in a market. It predicts that in a competitive market, price will function to equalize the quantity demanded by consumers, and the quantity supplied by producers, resulting in an economic equilibrium of price and quantity. The model incorporates other factors changing equilibrium as a shift of demand and/or supply.

   a. Joint demand
   b. Supply and demand
   c. Deferred gratification
   d. Rational addiction

18.

_____ was a German philosopher, political economist, historian, political theorist, sociologist, communist and revolutionary credited as the founder of communism.

Marx summarized his approach to history and politics in the opening line of the first chapter of The Communist Manifesto : e;The history of all hitherto existing society is the history of class struggles.e; Marx argued that capitalism, like previous socioeconomic systems, will produce internal tensions which will lead to its destruction. Just as capitalism replaced feudalism, socialism will in its turn replace capitalism and lead to a stateless, classless society which will emerge after a transitional period, the 'dictatorship of the proletariat'.

   a. Neo-Gramscianism
   b. Adam Smith
   c. Marxism
   d. Karl Heinrich Marx

19. In macroeconomics, _____ is a condition of the national economy, where all or nearly all persons willing and able to work at the prevailing wages and working conditions are able to do so. It is defined either as 0% unemployment, literally, no unemployment (the rate of unemployment is the fraction of the work force unable to find work), as by James Tobin, or as the level of employment rates when there is no cyclical unemployment. It is defined by the majority of mainstream economists as being an acceptable level of natural unemployment above 0%, the discrepancy from 0% being due to non-cyclical types of unemployment.

   a. Marginal propensity to consume
   b. Demand shock
   c. Harrod-Johnson diagram
   d. Full employment

Chapter 15. EMPLOYMENT AND UNEMPLOYMENT

20. In economics, _____ is a rise in the general level of prices of goods and services in an economy over a period of time. When the general price level rises, each unit of currency buys fewer goods and services; consequently, _____ is also a decline in the real value of money--a loss of purchasing power in the medium of exchange which is also the monetary unit of account in the economy. A chief measure of general price-level _____ is the general _____ rate, which is the percentage change in a general price index (normally the Consumer Price Index) over time.

   a. Inflation
   b. Economic
   c. Energy economics
   d. Opportunity cost

21. _____ is a broad label that refers to any individuals or households that use goods and services generated within the economy. The concept of a _____ is used in different contexts, so that the usage and significance of the term may vary.

Typically when business people and economists talk of _____s they are talking about person as _____, an aggregated commodity item with little individuality other than that expressed in the buy/not-buy decision.

   a. 1921 recession
   b. 130-30 fund
   c. 100-year flood
   d. Consumer

22. A _____ is a measure of the average price of consumer goods and services purchased by households. A _____ measures a price change for a constant market basket of goods and services from one period to the next within the same area (city, region, or nation.) It is a price index determined by measuring the price of a standard group of goods meant to represent the typical market basket of a typical urban consumer.

   a. Lipstick index
   b. Cost-of-living index
   c. CPI
   d. Consumer Price Index

23. _____ in economics and business is the result of an exchange and from that trade we assign a numerical monetary value to a good, service or asset. If Alice trades Bob 4 apples for an orange, the _____ of an orange is 4 apples. Inversely, the _____ of an apple is 1/4 oranges.

   a. Price book
   b. Premium pricing
   c. Price
   d. Price war

24. A _____ is a normalized average (typically a weighted average) of prices for a given class of goods or services in a given region, during a given interval of time. It is a statistic designed to help to compare how these prices, taken as a whole, differ between time periods or geographical locations.

Price indices have several potential uses.

   a. Price Index
   b. Transactional Net Margin Method
   c. Product sabotage
   d. Two-part tariff

25. _____ is sometimes referred to as _____, actually it means Economic Monetary Union.

Chapter 15. EMPLOYMENT AND UNEMPLOYMENT

First ideas of an economic and monetary union in Europe were raised well before establishing the European Communities. For example, already in the League of Nations, Gustav Stresemann asked in 1929 for a European currency (Link) against the background of an increased economic division due to a number of new nation states in Europe after WWI.

a. Exchange rate mechanism
b. European Monetary System
c. Euro Interbank Offered Rate
d. European Monetary Union

26. An economic and _____ is a single market with a common currency. It is to be distinguished from a mere currency union , which does not involve a single market. This is the fifth stage of economic integration.

a. Commercial invoice
b. Free trade zone
c. Customs union
d. Monetary Union

27. The term _____ refers to government debt, expenditures and revenues, or to finance (particularly financial revenue) in general.

- _____ deficit is the budget deficit of federal or local government
- _____ policy is the discretionary spending of governments. Contrasts with monetary policy.
- _____ year and _____ quarter are reporting periods for firms and other agencies.

a. Fiscal
b. Drawdown
c. Bucket shop
d. Procter ' Gamble

28. The term _____ refers to economy-wide fluctuations in production or economic activity over several months or years. These fluctuations occur around a long-term growth trend, and typically involve shifts over time between periods of relatively rapid economic growth (expansion or boom), and periods of relative stagnation or decline (contraction or recession.)

These fluctuations are often measured using the growth rate of real gross domestic product.

a. Nominal value
b. Consumer theory
c. Tobit model
d. Business cycle

Chapter 16. THE SUPPLY OF MONEY

1. The _____ is the central banking system of the United States. Created in 1913 by the enactment of the Federal Reserve Act (signed by Woodrow Wilson), it is a quasi-public and quasi-private (government entity with private components) banking system that comprises (1) the presidentially appointed Board of Governors of the _____ in Washington, D.C.; (2) the Federal Open Market Committee; (3) twelve regional Federal Reserve Banks located in major cities throughout the nation acting as fiscal agents for the U.S. Treasury, each with its own nine-member board of directors; (4) numerous other private U.S. member banks, which subscribe to required amounts of non-transferable stock in their regional Federal Reserve Banks; and (5) various advisory councils. Since February 2006, Ben Bernanke has served as the Chairman of the Board of Governors of the _____.

   a. Monetary Policy Report to the Congress
   b. Federal Reserve System
   c. Term auction facility
   d. Federal Reserve System Open Market Account

2. A _____ occurs when an entity spends more money than it takes in. The opposite of a _____ is a budget surplus. Debt is essentially an accumulated flow of deficits.

   a. Public Financial Management
   b. Lump-sum tax
   c. Funding body
   d. Budget deficit

3.

   A _____ is a type of financial intermediary and a type of bank. Commercial banking is also known as business banking. It is a bank that provides checking accounts, savings accounts, and money market accounts and that accepts time deposits.

   a. Bought deal
   b. Daylight overdraft
   c. Commercial bank
   d. Lombard banking

4. _____ was a survey conducted by the U.S. Department of Justice to gauge the prevalence of alcohol and illegal drug use among prior arrestees. It was a reformulation of the prior Drug Use Forecasting (DUF) program, focused on five drugs in particular: cocaine, marijuana, methamphetamine, opiates, and PCP.

   Participants were randomly selected from arrest records in major metropolitan areas; because no personally identifying information is taken from each record chosen, the resulting data can be correlated to arrest rates, but not to the total population of persons charged.

   a. ACEA agreement
   b. Arrestee Drug Abuse Monitoring
   c. ACCRA Cost of Living Index
   d. AD-IA Model

5. _____ is money declared by a government to be legal tender. The term derives from the Latin fiat, meaning 'let it be done'. _____ achieves value because a government accepts it in payment of taxes and says it can be used within the country as a 'tender' to pay all debts.

   a. Currency board
   b. Fiat money
   c. Devaluation
   d. World currency

Chapter 16. THE SUPPLY OF MONEY

6. Economics:

   - _____,the desire to own something and the ability to pay for it
   - _____ curve,a graphic representation of a _____ schedule
   - _____ deposit, the money in checking accounts
   - _____ pull theory,the theory that inflation occurs when _____ for goods and services exceeds existing supplies
   - _____ schedule,a table that lists the quantity of a good a person will buy it each different price
   - _____ side economics,the school of economics at believes government spending and tax cuts open economy by raising _____

   a. Variability
   c. McKesson ' Robbins scandal
   b. Demand
   d. Production

7. _____ is a type of bank account where the money in the account is legally able to be withdrawn immediately upon demand (or 'at call'.) This type of bank account can also be referred to as a 'cheque' or 'checking' or transactional account.

This type of bank account, allowing immediate conversion of the account balance into cash or withdrawal to another account, can be contrasted with a time deposit (also known as a certificate of deposit or term deposit), where the funds are not legally available for immediate withdrawal by the depositor.

   a. Debt rescheduling
   c. Clawbacks in economic development
   b. Tangible Common Equity
   d. Demand deposit

8. The accounting equation relates assets, _____, and owner's equity:

   Assets = _____ + Owner's Equity

The accounting equation is the mathematical structure of the balance sheet.

The Australian Accounting Research Foundation defines _____ as: 'future sacrifice of economic benefits that the entity is presently obliged to make to other entities as a result of past transactions and other past events.'

Probably the most accepted accounting definition of liability is the one used by the International Accounting Standards Board (IASB.) The following is a quotation from IFRS Framework:

A liability is a present obligation of the enterprise arising from past events, the settlement of which is expected to result in an outflow from the enterprise of resources embodying economic benefits

-

Regulations as to the recognition of _____ are different all over the world, but are roughly similar to those of the IASB.

Chapter 16. THE SUPPLY OF MONEY

a. Community property
b. Competition law theory
c. Coase theorem
d. Liabilities

9. The _____ is a group of three respected economists who advise the President of the United States on economic policy. It is a part of the Executive Office of the President of the United States, and provides much of the economic policy of the White House. The council prepares the annual Economic Report of the President.

a. Council of Economic Advisers
b. Hybrid renewable energy systems
c. Constrained Pareto optimality
d. Federal Reserve Bank Notes

10. _____s is the social science that studies the production, distribution, and consumption of goods and services. The term _____s comes from the Ancient Greek oá¼°κονομῑα from oá¼¶κος (oikos, 'house') + vĺŒμος (nomos, 'custom' or 'law'), hence 'rules of the house(hold)'. Current _____ models developed out of the broader field of political economy in the late 19th century, owing to a desire to use an empirical approach more akin to the physical sciences.

a. Opportunity cost
b. Energy economics
c. Inflation
d. Economic

11. _____ refers to the objective and subjective components of the believability of a source or message.

Traditionally, _____ has two key components: trustworthiness and expertise, which both have objective and subjective components. Trustworthiness is a based more on subjective factors, but can include objective measurements such as established reliability.

a. 130-30 fund
b. 100-year flood
c. 1921 recession
d. Credibility

12. The _____ is a bank regulation that sets the minimum reserves each bank must hold to customer deposits and notes. It would normally be in the form of fiat currency stored in a bank vault (vault cash), or with a central bank.

The reserve ratio is sometimes used as a tool in the monetary policy, influencing the country's economy, borrowing, and interest rates.

a. Probability of default
b. Fractional-reserve banking
c. Private money
d. Reserve requirement

13. _____ is sometimes referred to as _____, actually it means Economic Monetary Union.

First ideas of an economic and monetary union in Europe were raised well before establishing the European Communities. For example, already in the League of Nations, Gustav Stresemann asked in 1929 for a European currency (Link) against the background of an increased economic division due to a number of new nation states in Europe after WWI.

a. Euro Interbank Offered Rate
b. European Monetary System
c. Exchange rate mechanism
d. European Monetary Union

14. An economic and _____ is a single market with a common currency. It is to be distinguished from a mere currency union , which does not involve a single market. This is the fifth stage of economic integration.

Chapter 16. THE SUPPLY OF MONEY

a. Commercial invoice
b. Customs union
c. Free trade zone
d. Monetary Union

15. In banking, _____ are bank reserves in excess of the reserve requirement set by a central bank (in the United States, the Federal Reserve System, called the Fed; in Canada, the Bank of Canada.) They are reserves of cash more than the required amounts. Holding _____ is generally considered costly and uneconomical as no interest is earned on the excess amount.
   a. Annual percentage rate
   b. Universal bank
   c. Origination fee
   d. Excess reserves

16. A _____ is an expression that compares quantities relative to each other. The most common examples involve two quantities, but any number of quantities can be compared. _____s are represented mathematically by separating each quantity with a colon, for example the _____ 2:3, which is read as the _____ 'two to three'.
   a. 130-30 fund
   b. Ratio
   c. Y-intercept
   d. 100-year flood

17. The reserve requirement (or required _____) is a bank regulation that sets the minimum reserves each bank must hold to customer deposits and notes. It would normally be in the form of fiat currency stored in a bank vault (vault cash), or with a central bank.

The _____ is sometimes used as a tool in the monetary policy, influencing the country's economy, borrowing, and interest rates.

   a. Dividend unit
   b. First player wins
   c. Bank-State-Branch
   d. Reserve ratio

Chapter 16. THE SUPPLY OF MONEY 119

18. A _____ is:

- Rewrite _____, in generative grammar and computer science
- Standardization, a formal and widely-accepted statement, fact, definition, or qualification
- Operation, a determinate _____ for performing a mathematical operation and obtaining a certain result (Mathematics, Logic)
    - Unary operation
    - Binary operation
- _____ of inference, a function from sets of formulae to formulae (Mathematics, Logic)
- _____ of thumb, principle with broad application that is not intended to be strictly accurate or reliable for every situation. Also often simply referred to as a _____
- Moral, an atomic element of a moral code for guiding choices in human behavior
- Heuristic, a quantized '_____' which shows a tendency or probability for successful function
- A regulation, as in sports
- A Production _____, as in computer science
- Procedural law, a _____ set governing the application of laws to cases
    - A law, which may informally be called a '_____'
    - A court ruling, a decision by a court
- In the U.S. Government, a regulation mandated by Congress, but written or expanded upon by the Executive Branch.
- Norm (sociology), an informal but widely accepted _____, concept, truth, definition, or qualification (social norms, legal norms, coding norms)
- Norm (philosophy), a kind of sentence or a reason to act, feel or believe
- 'Rulership' is the concept of governance by a government:
    - Military _____, governance by a military body
    - Monastic _____, a collection of precepts that guides the life of monks or nuns in a religious order where the superior holds the place of Christ
- Slide _____

- '_____,' a song by Ayumi Hamasaki
- '_____,' a song by rapper Nas
- '_____s,' an album by the band The Whitest Boy Alive
- _____s: Pyaar Ka Superhit Formula, a 2003 Bollywood film
- ruler, an instrument for measuring lengths
- _____, a component of an astrolabe, circumferator or similar instrument
- The _____s, a bestselling self-help book
- _____ Project (Run Up-to-date Linux Everywhere), a project that aims to use up-to-date Linux software on old PCs
- _____ engine, a software system that helps managing business _____s
- Ja _____, a hip hop artist
    - R.U.L.E., a 2005 greatest hits album by rapper Ja _____
- '_____s,' a KMFDM song

a. Technocracy
c. Procter ' Gamble
b. Demand
d. Rule

Chapter 16. THE SUPPLY OF MONEY

19. In structured finance, a _____ is one of a number of related securities offered as part of the same transaction. The word _____ is French for slice, section, series, or portion. In the financial sense of the word, each bond is a different slice of the deal's risk.
   a. 130-30 fund
   b. 100-year flood
   c. Structured finance
   d. Tranche

20. The _____ consists of a number of economic theories which describe the nature of the firm, company including its existence, its behaviour, and its relationship with the market.

In simplified terms, the _____ aims to answer these questions:

  1. Existence - why do firms emerge, why are not all transactions in the economy mediated over the market?
  2. Boundaries - why the boundary between firms and the market is located exactly there? Which transactions are performed internally and which are negotiated on the market?
  3. Organization - why are firms structured in such specific way? What is the interplay of formal and informal relationships?

Despite looking simple, these questions are not answered by the established economic theory, which usually views firms as given, and treats them as black boxes without any internal structure.

The First World War period saw a change of emphasis in economic theory away from industry-level analysis which mainly included analysing markets to analysis at the level of the firm, as it became increasingly clear that perfect competition was no longer an adequate model of how firms behaved. Economic theory till then had focussed on trying to understand markets alone and there had been little study on understanding why firms or organisations exist.

   a. Technology gap
   b. Policy Ineffectiveness Proposition
   c. Khazzoom-Brookes postulate
   d. Theory of the firm

21. The _____ is a United States government corporation created by the Glass-Steagall Act of 1933. It provides deposit insurance, which guarantees the safety of deposits in member banks, currently up to $250,000 per depositor per bank. Funds in non-interest bearing transaction accounts are fully insured, with no limit, under the temporary Transaction Account Guarantee Program.
   a. Luxembourg Income Study
   b. Foreign direct investment
   c. Great Leap Forward
   d. Federal Deposit Insurance Corporation

22. _____, in law and economics, is a form of risk management primarily used to hedge against the risk of a contingent loss. _____ is defined as the equitable transfer of the risk of a loss, from one entity to another, in exchange for a premium, and can be thought of as a guaranteed small loss to prevent a large, possibly devastating loss. An insurer is a company selling the _____; an insured or policyholder is the person or entity buying the _____.
   a. ACEA agreement
   b. AD-IA Model
   c. ACCRA Cost of Living Index
   d. Insurance

Chapter 16. THE SUPPLY OF MONEY

23. Discounting is a financial mechanism in which a debtor obtains the right to delay payments to a creditor, for a defined period of time, in exchange for a charge or fee. Essentially, the party that owes money in the present purchases the right to delay the payment until some future date. The _____, or charge, is simply the difference between the original amount owed in the present and the amount that has to be paid in the future to settle the debt.
   a. Reliability theory
   b. Reinsurance
   c. Certified Risk Manager
   d. Discount

24. The _____ is an interest rate a central bank charges depository institutions that borrow reserves from it.

   The term _____ has two meanings:

   - the same as interest rate; the term 'discount' does not refer to the meaning of the word, but to the purpose of using the quantity, such as computations of present value, e.g. net present value or discounted cash flow

   - the annual effective _____, which is the annual interest divided by the capital including that interest; this rate is lower than the interest rate; it corresponds to using the value after a year as the nominal value, and seeing the initial value as the nominal value minus a discount; it is used for Treasury Bills and similar financial instruments

   The annual effective _____ is the annual interest divided by the capital including that interest, which is the interest rate divided by 100% plus the interest rate. It is the annual discount factor to be applied to the future cash flow, to find the discount, subtracted from a future value to find the value one year earlier.

   For example, suppose there is a government bond that sells for $95 and pays $100 in a year's time.

   a. Johansen test
   b. Perpetuity
   c. Stochastic volatility
   d. Discount rate

25. In finance, the term _____ describes various legal measures taken to ensure that debtors, whether individuals, businesses honor their debts and make an honest effort to repay the money that they owe. Generally regarded as a subdivision of tax law, _____ is most often enforced through a combination of audits and legal restrictions. For example, a provision of the Federal Debt Collection Procedure Act states that a person or organization indebted to the United States, against whom a judgment lien has been filed, is ineligible to receive a government grant.
   a. Debt compliance
   b. Microcredit
   c. Carryback loan
   d. Hard money loan

26. In economics, the _____ is the term used to refer to the environment in which bonds are bought and sold between a central bank ' its regulated banks. It is not a free market process.

   - To intervene in the 'business cycle', a central bank may choose to go into the _____ and buy or sell government bonds, which is known as _____ operations to increase reserves.

   a. Outside money
   b. Inside money
   c. ACCRA Cost of Living Index
   d. Open Market

Chapter 16. THE SUPPLY OF MONEY

27. In the United States, _____ are overnight borrowings by banks to maintain their bank reserves at the Federal Reserve. Banks keep reserves at Federal Reserve Banks to meet their reserve requirements and to clear financial transactions. Transactions in the _____ market enable depository institutions with reserve balances in excess of reserve requirements to lend reserves to institutions with reserve deficiencies.

- a. Federal funds rate
- b. Term auction facility
- c. Federal funds
- d. Federal Reserve Transparency Act

28. _____ are the means of implementing monetary policy by which a central bank controls its national money supply by buying and selling government securities, or other financial instruments. Monetary targets, such as interest rates or exchange rates, are used to guide this implementation.

Since most money is now in the form of electronic records, rather than paper records such as banknotes, _____ are conducted simply by electronically increasing or decreasing ('crediting' or 'debiting') the amount of money that a bank has, e.g., in its reserve account at the central bank, in exchange for a bank selling or buying a financial instrument.

- a. Open market operations
- b. ACCRA Cost of Living Index
- c. ACEA agreement
- d. AD-IA Model

29. The _____ , a component of the Federal Reserve System, is charged under United States law with overseeing the nation's open market operations. It is the Federal Reserve Committee that makes key decisions about interest rates and the growth jam of the United States money supply. It is the principal organ of United States national monetary policy.

- a. Fed Funds Probability
- b. Primary Dealer Credit Facility
- c. Federal Reserve Transparency Act
- d. Federal Open Market Committee

30. The _____ is a monetary system in which a region's common medium of exchange are paper notes that are normally freely convertible into pre-set, fixed quantities of gold. The _____ is not currently used by any government, having been replaced completely by fiat currency. Gold certificates were used as paper currency in the United States from 1882 to 1933, these certificates were freely convertable into gold coins.

In the 1790s Britain suffered a massive shortage of silver coinage and ceased to mint larger silver coins.

- a. 1921 recession
- b. 130-30 fund
- c. 100-year flood
- d. Gold standard

Chapter 17. MONETARY AND FISCAL POLICIES

1. _____s is the social science that studies the production, distribution, and consumption of goods and services. The term _____s comes from the Ancient Greek oá¼°κονομῑα from oá¼¶κος (oikos, 'house') + vΐŒμος (nomos, 'custom' or 'law'), hence 'rules of the house(hold)'. Current _____ models developed out of the broader field of political economy in the late 19th century, owing to a desire to use an empirical approach more akin to the physical sciences.
 a. Energy economics
 b. Opportunity cost
 c. Inflation
 d. Economic

2. _____ is a term used in economic research and policy debates. As with freedom generally, there are various definitions, but no universally accepted concept of _____. One major approach to _____ comes from the libertarian tradition emphasizing free markets and private property, while another extends the welfare economics study of individual choice, with greater _____ coming from a 'larger' (in some technical sense) set of possible choices.
 a. Economic liberalization
 b. Economic Freedom
 c. Investment policy
 d. International sanctions

3. The _____ was a worldwide economic downturn starting in most places in 1929 and ending at different times in the 1930s or early 1940s for different countries. It was the largest and most important economic depression in the 20th century, and is used in the 21st century as an example of how far the world's economy can fall. The _____ originated in the United States; historians most often use as a starting date the stock market crash on October 29, 1929, known as Black Tuesday.
 a. Wall Street Crash of 1929
 b. British Empire Economic Conference
 c. Jarrow March
 d. Great Depression

4. _____ was a global military conflict which involved a majority of the world's nations, including all of the great powers, organized into two opposing military alliances: the Allies and the Axis. The war involved the mobilization of over 100 million military personnel, making it the most widespread war in history. In a state of 'total war', the major participants placed their entire economic, industrial, and scientific capabilities at the service of the war effort, erasing the distinction between civilian and military resources.
 a. 130-30 fund
 b. 100-year flood
 c. 1921 recession
 d. World War II

5. Necessary _____s:

If x is a necessary _____ of y, then the presence of y necessarily implies the presence of x. The presence of x, however, does not imply that y will occur.

Sufficient _____s:

If x is a sufficient _____ of y, then the presence of x necessarily implies the presence of y.

 a. Political philosophy
 b. Materialism
 c. Cause
 d. Philosophy of economics

6. Manifesto of the Communist Party , often referred to as The _____, was first published on February 21, 1848, and is one of the world's most influential political manuscripts. Commissioned by the Communist League and written by communist theorists Karl Marx and Friedrich Engels, it laid out the League's purposes and program. It presents an analytical approach to the class struggle and the problems of capitalism, rather than a prediction of communism's potential future forms.

Chapter 17. MONETARY AND FISCAL POLICIES

a. Dialectical materialism
b. Labour power
c. Differential and Absolute Ground Rent
d. Communist Manifesto

7.

_____ was a German philosopher, political economist, historian, political theorist, sociologist, communist and revolutionary credited as the founder of communism.

Marx summarized his approach to history and politics in the opening line of the first chapter of The Communist Manifesto : e;The history of all hitherto existing society is the history of class struggles.e; Marx argued that capitalism, like previous socioeconomic systems, will produce internal tensions which will lead to its destruction. Just as capitalism replaced feudalism, socialism will in its turn replace capitalism and lead to a stateless, classless society which will emerge after a transitional period, the 'dictatorship of the proletariat'.

a. Marxism
b. Adam Smith
c. Karl Heinrich Marx
d. Neo-Gramscianism

8. In economics, a _____ is a general slowdown in economic activity over a sustained period of time, or a business cycle contraction. During _____s, many macroeconomic indicators vary in a similar way. Production as measured by Gross Domestic Product (GDP), employment, investment spending, capacity utilization, household incomes and business profits all fall during _____s.

a. Leading indicators
b. Monetary economics
c. Recession
d. Treasury View

9. In finance, the term _____ describes various legal measures taken to ensure that debtors, whether individuals, businesses honor their debts and make an honest effort to repay the money that they owe. Generally regarded as a subdivision of tax law, _____ is most often enforced through a combination of audits and legal restrictions. For example, a provision of the Federal Debt Collection Procedure Act states that a person or organization indebted to the United States, against whom a judgment lien has been filed, is ineligible to receive a government grant.

a. Microcredit
b. Hard money loan
c. Debt compliance
d. Carryback loan

10. _____ is a concept developed by the Austrian School of economics that refers to investments of firms being badly allocated due to artificially low cost of credit and an unsustainable increase in money supply, often blamed on a central bank.

This concept is central to the Austrian Business Cycle Theory.

a. Market neutral
b. Global Depository Receipt
c. Net domestic product
d. Malinvestment

11. The _____ is a group of three respected economists who advise the President of the United States on economic policy. It is a part of the Executive Office of the President of the United States, and provides much of the economic policy of the White House. The council prepares the annual Economic Report of the President.

a. Constrained Pareto optimality
b. Hybrid renewable energy systems
c. Federal Reserve Bank Notes
d. Council of Economic Advisers

Chapter 17. MONETARY AND FISCAL POLICIES

12. A _____ is a public holiday in both the United Kingdom and Ireland. There is some automatic right to time off on these days, although the majority of the population not employed in essential services (e.g. utilities, fire, ambulance, police, health-care workers, London Underground) receive them as holidays; those employed in essential services usually receive extra pay for working on these days. _____s are often assumed to be so called because they are days upon which banks are shut, but this is not in fact the case.
   a. 1921 recession
   c. 100-year flood
   b. 130-30 fund
   d. Bank holiday

13. A _____ refers to any type debt instrument, such as a loan, bond, mortgage that does not have a fixed rate of interest over the life of the instrument. Such debt typically uses an index or other base rate for establishing the interest rate for each relevant period. One of the most common rates to use as the basis for applying interest rates is the London Inter-bank Offered Rate, or LIBOR
   a. Moneylender
   c. Money market
   b. Floating interest rate
   d. Disposal tax effect

14. The _____ was an act signed into law on June 17, 1930, that raised U.S. tariffs on over 20,000 imported goods to record levels. In the United States 1,028 economists signed a petition against this legislation, and after it was passed, many countries retaliated with their own increased tariffs on U.S. goods, and American exports and imports were reduced by more than half.

Although rated capacity had increased tremendously, actual output, income, and expenditure had not.

   a. Smoot-Hawley Tariff Act
   c. Loss of use
   b. Judgment summons
   d. Patent Law Treaty

15. A _____ is a duty imposed on goods when they are moved across a political boundary. They are usually associated with protectionism, the economic policy of restraining trade between nations. For political reasons, _____s are usually imposed on imported goods, although they may also be imposed on exported goods.
   a. 100-year flood
   c. 1921 recession
   b. 130-30 fund
   d. Tariff

16. _____ is that which is owed; usually referencing assets owed, but the term can also cover moral obligations and other interactions not requiring money. In the case of assets, _____ is a means of using future purchasing power in the present before a summation has been earned. Some companies and corporations use _____ as a part of their overall corporate finance strategy.
   a. Collateral Management
   c. Debenture
   b. Hard money loan
   d. Debt

Chapter 17. MONETARY AND FISCAL POLICIES

17. Economics:

    - _____,the desire to own something and the ability to pay for it
    - _____ curve,a graphic representation of a _____ schedule
    - _____ deposit, the money in checking accounts
    - _____ pull theory,the theory that inflation occurs when _____ for goods and services exceeds existing supplies
    - _____ schedule,a table that lists the quantity of a good a person will buy it each different price
    - _____ side economics,the school of economics at believes government spending and tax cuts open economy by raising _____

    a. Variability
    c. Production
    b. McKesson ' Robbins scandal
    d. Demand

18. A _____ secures the proper functioning of money by regulating economic agents, transaction types, and money supply.

    _____s are traditionally formed by the policy decisions of individual governments and administrated as a domestic economic issue.

    The current trend, however, is to use international trade and investment to alter the policy and legislation of individual governments.

    a. Financial rand
    c. Consumer basket
    b. Netting
    d. Monetary system

19. _____ in economics and business is the result of an exchange and from that trade we assign a numerical monetary value to a good, service or asset. If Alice trades Bob 4 apples for an orange, the _____ of an orange is 4 apples. Inversely, the _____ of an apple is 1/4 oranges.

    a. Premium pricing
    c. Price
    b. Price book
    d. Price war

20. In economics, the _____ is that part of the economy which is both run for private profit and is not controlled by the state. By contrast, enterprises that are part of the state are part of the public sector; private, non-profit organizations are regarded as part of the voluntary sector.

    A variety of legal structures exist for _____ business organizations, depending on the jurisdiction in which they have their legal domicile.

    a. Standard Industrial Classification
    c. Primary products
    b. Secondary sector of the economy
    d. Private sector

21. The _____ is the part of economic and administrative life that deals with the delivery of goods and services by and for the government, whether national, regional or local/municipal.

Chapter 17. MONETARY AND FISCAL POLICIES

Examples of _____ activity range from delivering social security, administering urban planning and organising national defenses.

The organization of the _____ can take several forms, including:

- Direct administration funded through taxation; the delivering organization generally has no specific requirement to meet commercial success criteria, and production decisions are determined by government.
- Publicly owned corporations (in some contexts, especially manufacturing, 'state-owned enterprises'); which differ from direct administration in that they have greater commercial freedoms and are expected to operate according to commercial criteria, and production decisions are not generally taken by government (although goals may be set for them by government.)
- Partial outsourcing (of the scale many businesses do, e.g. for IT services), is considered a _____ model.

A borderline form is

- Complete outsourcing or contracting out, with a privately owned corporation delivering the entire service on behalf of government. This may be considered a mixture of private sector operations with public ownership of assets, although in some forms the private sector's control and/or risk is so great that the service may no longer be considered part of the _____.

a. 100-year flood
b. 130-30 fund
c. Policy cycle
d. Public sector

22. _____ refers to a business or organization attempting to acquire goods or services to accomplish the goals of the enterprise. Though there are several organizations that attempt to set standards in the _____ process, processes can vary greatly between organizations. Typically the word '_____' is not used interchangeably with the word 'procurement', since procurement typically includes Expediting, Supplier Quality, and Traffic and Logistics (T'L) in addition to _____.

a. 100-year flood
b. Free port
c. 130-30 fund
d. Purchasing

23. _____ is the number of goods/services that can be purchased with a unit of currency. For example, if you had taken one dollar to a store in the 1950s, you would have been able to buy a greater number of items than you would today, indicating that you would have had a greater _____ in the 1950s. Currency can be either a commodity money, like gold or silver, or fiat currency like US dollars.

a. Compliance cost
b. Human Poverty Index
c. Purchasing power
d. Genuine progress indicator

24. In business and accounting, _____ are everything of value that is owned by a person or company. It is a claim on the property your income of a borrower. The balance sheet of a firm records the monetary value of the _____ owned by the firm.

a. ACCRA Cost of Living Index
b. ACEA agreement
c. Amortization schedule
d. Assets

Chapter 17. MONETARY AND FISCAL POLICIES

25. The accounting equation relates assets, _____, and owner's equity:

   Assets = _____ + Owner's Equity

The accounting equation is the mathematical structure of the balance sheet.

The Australian Accounting Research Foundation defines _____ as: 'future sacrifice of economic benefits that the entity is presently obliged to make to other entities as a result of past transactions and other past events.'

Probably the most accepted accounting definition of liability is the one used by the International Accounting Standards Board (IASB.) The following is a quotation from IFRS Framework:

A liability is a present obligation of the enterprise arising from past events, the settlement of which is expected to result in an outflow from the enterprise of resources embodying economic benefits

-

Regulations as to the recognition of _____ are different all over the world, but are roughly similar to those of the IASB.

   a. Coase theorem
   c. Liabilities
   b. Competition law theory
   d. Community property

26. Market _____ is a business, economics or investment term that refers to an asset's ability to be easily converted through an act of buying or selling without causing a significant movement in the price and with minimum loss of value. Money, or cash on hand, is the most liquid asset. An act of exchange of a less liquid asset with a more liquid asset is called liquidation.
   a. 1921 recession
   c. 100-year flood
   b. 130-30 fund
   d. Liquidity

27. The _____ or gross domestic income (GDI), a basic measure of an economy's economic performance, is the market value of all final goods and services produced within the borders of a nation in a year. _____ can be defined in three ways, all of which are conceptually identical. First, it is equal to the total expenditures for all final goods and services produced within the country in a stipulated period of time (usually a 365-day year.)
   a. Countercyclical
   c. Gross domestic product
   b. Monopolistic competition
   d. Market structure

28. The _____ is one of several stock market indices, created by nineteenth-century Wall Street Journal editor and Dow Jones ' Company co-founder Charles Dow. It is an index that shows how certain stocks have traded. Dow compiled the index to gauge the performance of the industrial sector of the American stock market.
   a. Dow Jones Industrial Average
   c. Federal Reserve Bank Notes
   b. Fama-French three factor model
   d. Commodity fetishism

29. The _____ consists of a number of economic theories which describe the nature of the firm, company including its existence, its behaviour, and its relationship with the market.

Chapter 17. MONETARY AND FISCAL POLICIES

In simplified terms, the _____ aims to answer these questions:

1. Existence - why do firms emerge, why are not all transactions in the economy mediated over the market?
2. Boundaries - why the boundary between firms and the market is located exactly there? Which transactions are performed internally and which are negotiated on the market?
3. Organization - why are firms structured in such specific way? What is the interplay of formal and informal relationships?

Despite looking simple, these questions are not answered by the established economic theory, which usually views firms as given, and treats them as black boxes without any internal structure.

The First World War period saw a change of emphasis in economic theory away from industry-level analysis which mainly included analysing markets to analysis at the level of the firm, as it became increasingly clear that perfect competition was no longer an adequate model of how firms behaved. Economic theory till then had focussed on trying to understand markets alone and there had been little study on understanding why firms or organisations exist.

a. Policy Ineffectiveness Proposition
b. Khazzoom-Brookes postulate
c. Theory of the firm
d. Technology gap

30. The _____ is a United States government corporation created by the Glass-Steagall Act of 1933. It provides deposit insurance, which guarantees the safety of deposits in member banks, currently up to $250,000 per depositor per bank. Funds in non-interest bearing transaction accounts are fully insured, with no limit, under the temporary Transaction Account Guarantee Program.

a. Luxembourg Income Study
b. Foreign direct investment
c. Great Leap Forward
d. Federal Deposit Insurance Corporation

31. _____, in law and economics, is a form of risk management primarily used to hedge against the risk of a contingent loss. _____ is defined as the equitable transfer of the risk of a loss, from one entity to another, in exchange for a premium, and can be thought of as a guaranteed small loss to prevent a large, possibly devastating loss. An insurer is a company selling the _____; an insured or policyholder is the person or entity buying the _____.

a. AD-IA Model
b. ACEA agreement
c. ACCRA Cost of Living Index
d. Insurance

32. In economics, the _____ is the term used to refer to the environment in which bonds are bought and sold between a central bank ' its regulated banks. It is not a free market process.

- To intervene in the 'business cycle', a central bank may choose to go into the _____ and buy or sell government bonds, which is known as _____ operations to increase reserves.

a. Outside money
b. Open Market
c. Inside money
d. ACCRA Cost of Living Index

Chapter 17. MONETARY AND FISCAL POLICIES

33. In the United States, _____ are overnight borrowings by banks to maintain their bank reserves at the Federal Reserve. Banks keep reserves at Federal Reserve Banks to meet their reserve requirements and to clear financial transactions. Transactions in the _____ market enable depository institutions with reserve balances in excess of reserve requirements to lend reserves to institutions with reserve deficiencies.
   a. Federal funds rate
   b. Term auction facility
   c. Federal funds
   d. Federal Reserve Transparency Act

34. In the United States, the _____ is the interest rate at which private depository institutions (mostly banks) lend balances (federal funds) at the Federal Reserve to other depository institutions, usually overnight. It is the interest rate banks charge each other for loans. Changing the target rate is one way the Chairman of the Federal Reserve can influence the supply of money in the U.S. economy..
   a. Monetary Policy Report to the Congress
   b. Federal funds rate
   c. Term auction facility
   d. Federal banking

35. _____ is the process by which the government, central bank (ii) availability of money, and (iii) cost of money or rate of interest, in order to attain a set of objectives oriented towards the growth and stability of the economy. Monetary theory provides insight into how to craft optimal _____.

   _____ is referred to as either being an expansionary policy where an expansionary policy increases the total supply of money in the economy, and a contractionary policy decreases the total money supply.

   a. 100-year flood
   b. Monetary policy
   c. 1921 recession
   d. 130-30 fund

36. _____ was a survey conducted by the U.S. Department of Justice to gauge the prevalence of alcohol and illegal drug use among prior arrestees. It was a reformulation of the prior Drug Use Forecasting (DUF) program, focused on five drugs in particular: cocaine, marijuana, methamphetamine, opiates, and PCP.

   Participants were randomly selected from arrest records in major metropolitan areas; because no personally identifying information is taken from each record chosen, the resulting data can be correlated to arrest rates, but not to the total population of persons charged.

   a. ACEA agreement
   b. Arrestee Drug Abuse Monitoring
   c. ACCRA Cost of Living Index
   d. AD-IA Model

37. _____, often referred to by his initials _____, was the 32nd President of the United States. He was a central figure of the 20th century during a time of worldwide economic crisis and world war. Elected to four terms in office, he served from 1933 to 1945 and is the only U.S. president to have served more than two terms.
   a. Adolf Hitler
   b. Adolph Fischer
   c. Franklin Delano Roosevelt
   d. Adam Smith

38. _____ is the socio-economic status of unfree peasants under feudalism, and specifically relates to Manorialism. It was a condition of bondage or modified slavery which developed primarily during the High Middle Ages in Europe. _____ was the enforced labour of serfs on the fields of landowners, in return for protection and the right to work on their leased fields.

Chapter 17. MONETARY AND FISCAL POLICIES

a. Landwirtschaftliche Produktionsgenossenschaft
b. Rural tenancy
c. Serfdom
d. Metayage

39. The term _____ refers to government debt, expenditures and revenues, or to finance (particularly financial revenue) in general.

- _____ deficit is the budget deficit of federal or local government
- _____ policy is the discretionary spending of governments. Contrasts with monetary policy.
- _____ year and _____ quarter are reporting periods for firms and other agencies.

a. Procter ' Gamble
b. Bucket shop
c. Drawdown
d. Fiscal

40. In economics, _____ is the use of government spending and revenue collection to influence the economy.

_____ can be contrasted with the other main type of economic policy, monetary policy, which attempts to stabilize the economy by controlling interest rates and the supply of money. The two main instruments of _____ are government spending and taxation.

a. 100-year flood
b. Fiscalism
c. Fiscal policy
d. Sustainable investment rule

41. _____, 1st Baron Keynes was a renowned economist from Britain whose many ideas on economic and political theories as well as on many governments' monetary policies influenced America. He advocated a government that played an active role in the lives of people regarding business, economy, etc. In this role, the government would use fiscal measures to reduce the consequences of recessions, economic depressions and booms.

a. Adolph Fischer
b. Adam Smith
c. Adolf Hitler
d. John Maynard Keynes

42. The _____ was written by Adam Smith in 1759. It provided the ethical, philosophical, psychological and methodological underpinnings to Smith's later works, including The Wealth of Nations (1776), A Treatise on Public Opulence (1764) (first published in 1937), Essays on Philosophical Subjects (1795), and Lectures on Justice, Police, Revenue, and Arms (1763) (first published in 1896.)

Broadly speaking, Smith followed the views of his mentor, Francis Hutcheson of the University of Glasgow, who divided moral philosophy into four parts: Ethics and Virtue; Private rights and Natural liberty; Familial rights (called Economics); and State and Individual rights (called Politics.)

a. Capital and Interest
b. Butterfly Economics
c. Theory of Moral Sentiments
d. Limits to Growth

43. Many _____ are related to the environmental consequences of production and use

- Systemic risk describes the risks to the overall economy arising from the risks which the banking system takes. That the private costs of banking failure may be smaller than the social costs justifies banking regulations, although regulations could create a moral hazard.

- Anthropogenic climate change is attributed to greenhouse gas emissions from burning oil, gas, and coal. Global warming has been ranked as the #1 externality of all economic activity, in the magnitude of potential harms and yet remains unmitigated.

a. White certificates
c. Green certificate
b. Negative externalities
d. Total Economic Value

44. Examples of _____ include:

- A beekeeper keeps the bees for their honey. A side effect or externality associated with his activity is the pollination of surrounding crops by the bees. The value generated by the pollination may be more important than the value of the harvested honey.

- An individual planting an attractive garden in front of his house may provide benefits to others living in the area, and even financial benefits in the form of increased property values for all property owners.

- An individual buying a product that is interconnected in a network (e.g., a video cellphone) will increase the usefulness of such phones to other people who have a video cellphone. When each new user of a product increases the value of the same product owned by others, the phenomenon is called a network externality or a network effect. Network externalities often have 'tipping points' where, suddenly, the product reaches general acceptance and near-universal usage, a phenomenon which can be seen in the near universal take-up of cellphones in some Scandinavian countries.

- Knowledge spillover of inventions and information - once an invention (or most other forms of practical information) is discovered or made more easily accessible, others benefit by exploiting the invention or information. Copyright and intellectual property law are mechanisms to allow the inventor or creator to benefit from a temporary, state-protected monopoly in return for 'sharing' the information through publication or other means.

a. Total Economic Value
c. Positive externalities
b. Weighted average cost of carbon
d. Negative externalities

45. A _____ is a package or set of measures introduced to stabilise a financial system or economy. The term can refer to policies in two distinct sets of circumstances: business cycle stabilization and crisis stabilization.

Stabilization can refer to correcting the normal behavior of the business cycle.

a. Capacity Development
c. Stabilization policy
b. New International Economic Order
d. Volunteers for Economic Growth Alliance

Chapter 18. ECONOMIC PERFORMANCE AND POLITICAL ECONOMY

1. _____s is the social science that studies the production, distribution, and consumption of goods and services. The term _____s comes from the Ancient Greek oá¼°κονομῖα from oá¼¶κος (oikos, 'house') + vÏŒμος (nomos, 'custom' or 'law'), hence 'rules of the house(hold)'. Current _____ models developed out of the broader field of political economy in the late 19th century, owing to a desire to use an empirical approach more akin to the physical sciences.

   a. Economic
   b. Inflation
   c. Energy economics
   d. Opportunity cost

2. _____ is a term used in economic research and policy debates. As with freedom generally, there are various definitions, but no universally accepted concept of _____. One major approach to _____ comes from the libertarian tradition emphasizing free markets and private property, while another extends the welfare economics study of individual choice, with greater _____ coming from a 'larger' (in some technical sense) set of possible choices.

   a. Economic Freedom
   b. Investment policy
   c. International sanctions
   d. Economic liberalization

3. A _____ occurs when an entity spends more money than it takes in. The opposite of a _____ is a budget surplus. Debt is essentially an accumulated flow of deficits.

   a. Public Financial Management
   b. Funding body
   c. Lump-sum tax
   d. Budget deficit

4. In finance, the term _____ describes various legal measures taken to ensure that debtors, whether individuals, businesses honor their debts and make an honest effort to repay the money that they owe. Generally regarded as a subdivision of tax law, _____ is most often enforced through a combination of audits and legal restrictions. For example, a provision of the Federal Debt Collection Procedure Act states that a person or organization indebted to the United States, against whom a judgment lien has been filed, is ineligible to receive a government grant.

   a. Debt compliance
   b. Hard money loan
   c. Microcredit
   d. Carryback loan

5. _____ originally was the term for studying production, buying and selling, and their relations with law, custom, and government. _____ originated in moral philosophy. It developed in the 18th century as the study of the economies of states -- polities, hence _____.

   a. Dirigisme
   b. Political economy
   c. Geoeconomics
   d. Productive and unproductive labour

6. The _____ was written by Adam Smith in 1759. It provided the ethical, philosophical, psychological and methodological underpinnings to Smith's later works, including The Wealth of Nations (1776), A Treatise on Public Opulence (1764) (first published in 1937), Essays on Philosophical Subjects (1795), and Lectures on Justice, Police, Revenue, and Arms (1763) (first published in 1896.)

Broadly speaking, Smith followed the views of his mentor, Francis Hutcheson of the University of Glasgow, who divided moral philosophy into four parts: Ethics and Virtue; Private rights and Natural liberty; Familial rights (called Economics); and State and Individual rights (called Politics.)

   a. Limits to Growth
   b. Butterfly Economics
   c. Capital and Interest
   d. Theory of Moral Sentiments

Chapter 18. ECONOMIC PERFORMANCE AND POLITICAL ECONOMY

7. _____ is a broad label that refers to any individuals or households that use goods and services generated within the economy. The concept of a _____ is used in different contexts, so that the usage and significance of the term may vary.

Typically when business people and economists talk of _____s they are talking about person as _____, an aggregated commodity item with little individuality other than that expressed in the buy/not-buy decision.

   a. Consumer
   c. 100-year flood
   b. 130-30 fund
   d. 1921 recession

8. A _____ is a measure of the average price of consumer goods and services purchased by households. A _____ measures a price change for a constant market basket of goods and services from one period to the next within the same area (city, region, or nation.) It is a price index determined by measuring the price of a standard group of goods meant to represent the typical market basket of a typical urban consumer.
   a. Lipstick index
   c. Cost-of-living index
   b. CPI
   d. Consumer Price Index

9. _____ is sometimes referred to as _____, actually it means Economic Monetary Union.

First ideas of an economic and monetary union in Europe were raised well before establishing the European Communities. For example, already in the League of Nations, Gustav Stresemann asked in 1929 for a European currency (Link) against the background of an increased economic division due to a number of new nation states in Europe after WWI.

   a. European Monetary System
   c. Exchange rate mechanism
   b. European Monetary Union
   d. Euro Interbank Offered Rate

10. An economic and _____ is a single market with a common currency. It is to be distinguished from a mere currency union, which does not involve a single market. This is the fifth stage of economic integration.
   a. Commercial invoice
   c. Customs union
   b. Free trade zone
   d. Monetary Union

11. _____ in economics and business is the result of an exchange and from that trade we assign a numerical monetary value to a good, service or asset. If Alice trades Bob 4 apples for an orange, the _____ of an orange is 4 apples. Inversely, the _____ of an apple is 1/4 oranges.
   a. Price war
   c. Premium pricing
   b. Price book
   d. Price

12. A _____ is a normalized average (typically a weighted average) of prices for a given class of goods or services in a given region, during a given interval of time. It is a statistic designed to help to compare how these prices, taken as a whole, differ between time periods or geographical locations.

Price indices have several potential uses.

Chapter 18. ECONOMIC PERFORMANCE AND POLITICAL ECONOMY 135

a. Two-part tariff
b. Transactional Net Margin Method
c. Price Index
d. Product sabotage

13. The term _____ refers to government debt, expenditures and revenues, or to finance (particularly financial revenue) in general.

- _____ deficit is the budget deficit of federal or local government
- _____ policy is the discretionary spending of governments. Contrasts with monetary policy.
- _____ year and _____ quarter are reporting periods for firms and other agencies.

a. Procter ' Gamble
b. Drawdown
c. Fiscal
d. Bucket shop

14. _____ was a survey conducted by the U.S. Department of Justice to gauge the prevalence of alcohol and illegal drug use among prior arrestees. It was a reformulation of the prior Drug Use Forecasting (DUF) program, focused on five drugs in particular: cocaine, marijuana, methamphetamine, opiates, and PCP.

Participants were randomly selected from arrest records in major metropolitan areas; because no personally identifying information is taken from each record chosen, the resulting data can be correlated to arrest rates, but not to the total population of persons charged.

a. ACEA agreement
b. Arrestee Drug Abuse Monitoring
c. ACCRA Cost of Living Index
d. AD-IA Model

15. The _____ is a group of three respected economists who advise the President of the United States on economic policy. It is a part of the Executive Office of the President of the United States, and provides much of the economic policy of the White House. The council prepares the annual Economic Report of the President.

a. Constrained Pareto optimality
b. Federal Reserve Bank Notes
c. Hybrid renewable energy systems
d. Council of Economic Advisers

16. _____ is a term used in economics to describe how an economic quantity is related to economic fluctuations. It is the opposite of procyclical. However, it has more than one meaning.

a. Law of comparative advantage
b. Countercyclical
c. Price revolution
d. Mathematical economics

17. In economics, _____ is the use of government spending and revenue collection to influence the economy.

_____ can be contrasted with the other main type of economic policy, monetary policy, which attempts to stabilize the economy by controlling interest rates and the supply of money. The two main instruments of _____ are government spending and taxation.

a. Fiscal policy
b. Sustainable investment rule
c. Fiscalism
d. 100-year flood

Chapter 18. ECONOMIC PERFORMANCE AND POLITICAL ECONOMY

18. The _____ was a worldwide economic downturn starting in most places in 1929 and ending at different times in the 1930s or early 1940s for different countries. It was the largest and most important economic depression in the 20th century, and is used in the 21st century as an example of how far the world's economy can fall. The _____ originated in the United States; historians most often use as a starting date the stock market crash on October 29, 1929, known as Black Tuesday.
  a. British Empire Economic Conference
  b. Wall Street Crash of 1929
  c. Jarrow March
  d. Great Depression

19. _____ and Keynesian Theory) is a macroeconomic theory based on the ideas of 20th-century British economist John Maynard Keynes. _____ argues that private sector decisions sometimes lead to inefficient macroeconomic outcomes and therefore advocates active policy responses by the public sector, including monetary policy actions by the central bank and fiscal policy actions by the government to stabilize output over the business cycle.

The theories forming the basis of _____ were first presented in The General Theory of Employment, Interest and Money, published in 1936.

  a. Market failure
  b. Deflation
  c. Keynesian economics
  d. Rational choice theory

20. _____, often referred to by his initials _____, was the 32nd President of the United States. He was a central figure of the 20th century during a time of worldwide economic crisis and world war. Elected to four terms in office, he served from 1933 to 1945 and is the only U.S. president to have served more than two terms.
  a. Franklin Delano Roosevelt
  b. Adolph Fischer
  c. Adam Smith
  d. Adolf Hitler

21. _____ is the socio-economic status of unfree peasants under feudalism, and specifically relates to Manorialism. It was a condition of bondage or modified slavery which developed primarily during the High Middle Ages in Europe. _____ was the enforced labour of serfs on the fields of landowners, in return for protection and the right to work on their leased fields.
  a. Serfdom
  b. Landwirtschaftliche Produktionsgenossenschaft
  c. Metayage
  d. Rural tenancy

22. _____ was a Scottish moral philosopher and a pioneer of political economy. One of the key figures of the Scottish Enlightenment, Smith is the author of The Theory of Moral Sentiments and An Inquiry into the Nature and Causes of the Wealth of Nations. The latter, usually abbreviated as The Wealth of Nations, is considered his magnum opus and the first modern work of economics.
  a. Adam Smith
  b. Adolph Fischer
  c. Alan Greenspan
  d. Adolf Hitler

23. The term _____ refers to economy-wide fluctuations in production or economic activity over several months or years. These fluctuations occur around a long-term growth trend, and typically involve shifts over time between periods of relatively rapid economic growth (expansion or boom), and periods of relative stagnation or decline (contraction or recession.)

These fluctuations are often measured using the growth rate of real gross domestic product.

Chapter 18. ECONOMIC PERFORMANCE AND POLITICAL ECONOMY 137

a. Business cycle
b. Nominal value
c. Tobit model
d. Consumer theory

24. In economics, _____ is inflation that is very high or 'out of control', a condition in which prices increase rapidly as a currency loses its value. Definitions used by the media vary from a cumulative inflation rate over three years approaching 100% to 'inflation exceeding 50% a month.' In informal usage the term is often applied to much lower rates. As a rule of thumb, normal inflation is reported per year, but _____ is often reported for much shorter intervals, often per month.

a. 100-year flood
b. 130-30 fund
c. 1921 recession
d. Hyperinflation

25. _____ is the process by which the government, central bank (ii) availability of money, and (iii) cost of money or rate of interest, in order to attain a set of objectives oriented towards the growth and stability of the economy. Monetary theory provides insight into how to craft optimal _____.

_____ is referred to as either being an expansionary policy where an expansionary policy increases the total supply of money in the economy, and a contractionary policy decreases the total money supply.

a. 130-30 fund
b. 100-year flood
c. Monetary policy
d. 1921 recession

26. An _____ or Ä"conomic system is a system that involves the production, distribution and consumption of goods and services between the entities in a particular society. It is the method used by society to produce and distribute goods and services. The _____ is composed of people and institutions, including their relationships to productive resources, such as through the convention of property.

a. Information economy
b. Indicative planning
c. Intention economy
d. Economic system

27. _____, 1st Baron Keynes was a renowned economist from Britain whose many ideas on economic and political theories as well as on many governments' monetary policies influenced America. He advocated a government that played an active role in the lives of people regarding business, economy, etc. In this role, the government would use fiscal measures to reduce the consequences of recessions, economic depressions and booms.

a. Adolf Hitler
b. Adolph Fischer
c. John Maynard Keynes
d. Adam Smith

28.

_____ was a German philosopher, political economist, historian, political theorist, sociologist, communist and revolutionary credited as the founder of communism.

Marx summarized his approach to history and politics in the opening line of the first chapter of The Communist Manifesto : e;The history of all hitherto existing society is the history of class struggles.e; Marx argued that capitalism, like previous socioeconomic systems, will produce internal tensions which will lead to its destruction. Just as capitalism replaced feudalism, socialism will in its turn replace capitalism and lead to a stateless, classless society which will emerge after a transitional period, the 'dictatorship of the proletariat'.

Chapter 18. ECONOMIC PERFORMANCE AND POLITICAL ECONOMY

a. Marxism
b. Neo-Gramscianism
c. Karl Heinrich Marx
d. Adam Smith

29. _____ is an economic system in which wealth, and the means of producing wealth, are privately owned. Through _____, the land, labor, and capital are owned, operated, and traded for the purpose of generating profits, without force or fraud, by private individuals either singly or jointly, and investments, distribution, income, production, pricing and supply of goods, commodities and services are determined by voluntary private decision in a market economy. A distinguishing feature of _____ is that each person owns his or her own labor and therefore is allowed to sell the use of it to employers.

a. Late capitalism
b. Creative capitalism
c. Socialism for the rich and capitalism for the poor
d. Capitalism

30. _____ is the political philosophy and practice derived from the work of Karl Marx and Friedrich Engels. _____ holds at its core a critical analysis of capitalism and a theory of social change. The powerful and innovative methods of analysis introduced by Marx have been very influential in a broad range of disciplines.

a. Neo-Gramscianism
b. Karl Heinrich Marx
c. Adam Smith
d. Marxism

31. _____ was the theoretical journal of the Communist Party of Great Britain and was dissolved in 1991. It was particularly important during the 1980s under the editorship of Martin Jacques. Through _____ Jacques, amongst others, coined the term Thatcherism and believed they were deconstructing the ideology of the government of the then Prime Minister of the United Kingdom, Margaret Thatcher, through their theory of New Times.

a. 100-year flood
b. 1921 recession
c. 130-30 fund
d. Marxism Today

32. _____ in political thought refers to economic theories of social organization advocating collective ownership and administration of the means of production and distribution of goods, and a society characterized by equality for all individuals, with an egalitarian method of compensation. Modern _____ originated in the late 19th-century intellectual and working class political movement that criticized the effects of industrialization and private ownership on society. Karl Marx posited that _____ would be achieved via class struggle and a proletarian revolution after a transitional stage from capitalism called the dictatorship of the proletariat.

a. Adam Smith
b. Socialism
c. Adolf Hitler
d. Adolph Fischer

33. The _____ is an international organization that oversees the global financial system by following the macroeconomic policies of its member countries, in particular those with an impact on exchange rates and the balance of payments. It is an organization formed to stabilize international exchange rates and facilitate development. It also offers financial and technical assistance to its members, making it an international lender of last resort.

a. Office of Thrift Supervision
b. ACCRA Cost of Living Index
c. ACEA agreement
d. International Monetary Fund

34. An Inquiry into the Nature and Causes of the _____ is the magnum opus of the Scottish economist Adam Smith. It is a clearly written account of economics at the dawn of the Industrial Revolution, as well as a rhetorical piece written for the generally educated individual of the 18th century - advocating a free market economy as more productive and more beneficial to society.

Chapter 18. ECONOMIC PERFORMANCE AND POLITICAL ECONOMY

The work is credited as a watershed in history and economics due to its comprehensive, largely accurate characterization of economic mechanisms that survive in modern economics; and also for its effective use of rhetorical technique, including structuring the work to contrast real world examples of free and fettered markets.

- a. The Rise and Fall of the Great Powers
- b. Black Book of Communism
- c. The Bell Curve
- d. Wealth of Nations

35. In finance, the _____s between two currencies specifies how much one currency is worth in terms of the other. It is the value of a foreign natione;s currency in terms of the home natione;s currency. For example an _____ of 102 Japanese yen to the United States dollar means that JPY 102 is worth the same as USD 1.
- a. Exchange rate
- b. ACCRA Cost of Living Index
- c. Interbank market
- d. ACEA agreement

36. A _____ is any systematic process enabling many market players to bid and ask: helping bidders and sellers interact and make deals. It is not just the price mechanism but the entire system of regulation, qualification, credentials, reputations and clearing that surrounds that mechanism and makes it operate in a social context.

Because a _____ relies on the assumption that players are constantly involved and unequally enabled, a _____ is distinguished specifically from a voting system where candidates seek the support of voters on a less regular basis.

- a. Price mechanism
- b. Contestable market
- c. Market system
- d. Competitive equilibrium

37. A fixed exchange rate, sometimes called a _____, is a type of exchange rate regime wherein a currency's value is matched to the value of another single currency or to a basket of other currencies such as gold.

A fixed exchange rate is usually used to stabilize the value of a currency, vis-a-vis the currency it is pegged to. This facilitates trade and investments between the two countries, and is especially useful for small economies where external trade forms a large part of their GDP.

- a. Leading indicators
- b. Recession
- c. Mainstream economics
- d. Pegged exchange rate

Chapter 19. NATIONAL POLICIES AND INTERNATIONAL EXCHANGE

1. _____ was a survey conducted by the U.S. Department of Justice to gauge the prevalence of alcohol and illegal drug use among prior arrestees. It was a reformulation of the prior Drug Use Forecasting (DUF) program, focused on five drugs in particular: cocaine, marijuana, methamphetamine, opiates, and PCP.

Participants were randomly selected from arrest records in major metropolitan areas; because no personally identifying information is taken from each record chosen, the resulting data can be correlated to arrest rates, but not to the total population of persons charged.

   a. ACCRA Cost of Living Index
   b. Arrestee Drug Abuse Monitoring
   c. AD-IA Model
   d. ACEA agreement

2. _____s is the social science that studies the production, distribution, and consumption of goods and services. The term _____s comes from the Ancient Greek oá¼°κονομῖα from oá¼¶κος (oikos, 'house') + vÏŒμος (nomos, 'custom' or 'law'), hence 'rules of the house(hold)'. Current _____ models developed out of the broader field of political economy in the late 19th century, owing to a desire to use an empirical approach more akin to the physical sciences.
   a. Inflation
   b. Energy economics
   c. Opportunity cost
   d. Economic

3. _____ is sometimes referred to as _____, actually it means Economic Monetary Union.

First ideas of an economic and monetary union in Europe were raised well before establishing the European Communities. For example, already in the League of Nations, Gustav Stresemann asked in 1929 for a European currency (Link) against the background of an increased economic division due to a number of new nation states in Europe after WWI.

   a. Exchange rate mechanism
   b. Euro Interbank Offered Rate
   c. European Monetary System
   d. European Monetary Union

4. _____ is a term used to collectively describe topics relating to the operations of firms with interests in multiple countries. Such firms are sometimes called multinational corporations. Well known MNCs include fast food companies McDonald's and Yum Brands, vehicle manufacturers such as General Motors and Toyota, consumer electronics companies like Samsung, LG and Sony, and energy companies such as ExxonMobil and BP.
   a. ACEA agreement
   b. AD-IA Model
   c. International Business
   d. ACCRA Cost of Living Index

5. The _____ is an international organization that oversees the global financial system by following the macroeconomic policies of its member countries, in particular those with an impact on exchange rates and the balance of payments. It is an organization formed to stabilize international exchange rates and facilitate development. It also offers financial and technical assistance to its members, making it an international lender of last resort.
   a. ACCRA Cost of Living Index
   b. ACEA agreement
   c. Office of Thrift Supervision
   d. International Monetary Fund

6. An economic and _____ is a single market with a common currency. It is to be distinguished from a mere currency union, which does not involve a single market. This is the fifth stage of economic integration.
   a. Free trade zone
   b. Customs union
   c. Commercial invoice
   d. Monetary Union

Chapter 19. NATIONAL POLICIES AND INTERNATIONAL EXCHANGE

7. The _____ is a US private, nonprofit research organization dedicated to studying the science and empirics of economics, especially the American economy. It is 'committed to undertaking and disseminating unbiased economic research among public policymakers, business professionals, and the academic community.' It publishes NBER Working Papers and books. The NBER is located in Cambridge, Massachusetts with branch offices in Palo Alto, California, and New York City.
   a. CEFTA
   b. Non-governmental organization
   c. National Bureau of Economic Research
   d. Deutsche Bank

8. _____ was a Scottish moral philosopher and a pioneer of political economy. One of the key figures of the Scottish Enlightenment, Smith is the author of The Theory of Moral Sentiments and An Inquiry into the Nature and Causes of the Wealth of Nations. The latter, usually abbreviated as The Wealth of Nations, is considered his magnum opus and the first modern work of economics.
   a. Adolf Hitler
   b. Alan Greenspan
   c. Adolph Fischer
   d. Adam Smith

9. _____ or amortisation is the process of increasing an amount over a period of time. The word comes from Middle English amortisen to kill, alienate in mortmain, from Anglo-French amorteser, alteration of amortir, from Vulgar Latin admortire to kill, from Latin ad- + mort-, mors death. Particular instances of the term include:

   - _____, the allocation of a lump sum amount to different time periods, particularly for loans and other forms of finance, including related interest or other finance charges.
      o _____ schedule, a table detailing each periodic payment on a loan (typically a mortgage), as generated by an _____ calculator.
      o Negative _____, an _____ schedule where the loan amount actually increases through not paying the full interest
   - Amortized analysis, analyzing the execution cost of algorithms over a sequence of operations.
   - _____ of capital expenditures of certain assets under accounting rules, particularly intangible assets, in a manner analogous to depreciation.
   - _____ (tax law)

_____ is also used in the context of zoning regulations and describes the time in which a property owner has to relocate when the property's use constitutes a preexisting nonconforming use under zoning regulations.

   a. Augmentation
   b. Oslo Agreements
   c. Economic miracle
   d. Amortization

10. The _____ is a group of three respected economists who advise the President of the United States on economic policy. It is a part of the Executive Office of the President of the United States, and provides much of the economic policy of the White House. The council prepares the annual Economic Report of the President.
    a. Hybrid renewable energy systems
    b. Federal Reserve Bank Notes
    c. Constrained Pareto optimality
    d. Council of Economic Advisers

11. A _____ refers to any type debt instrument, such as a loan, bond, mortgage that does not have a fixed rate of interest over the life of the instrument. Such debt typically uses an index or other base rate for establishing the interest rate for each relevant period. One of the most common rates to use as the basis for applying interest rates is the London Inter-bank Offered Rate, or LIBOR

a. Moneylender
b. Disposal tax effect
c. Floating interest rate
d. Money market

12. _____ is that which is owed; usually referencing assets owed, but the term can also cover moral obligations and other interactions not requiring money. In the case of assets, _____ is a means of using future purchasing power in the present before a summation has been earned. Some companies and corporations use _____ as a part of their overall corporate finance strategy.
 a. Hard money loan
 b. Debt
 c. Collateral Management
 d. Debenture

13. In economics, an _____ is any good or commodity, transported from one country to another country in a legitimate fashion, typically for use in trade. _____ goods or services are provided to foreign consumers by domestic producers. _____ is an important part of international trade.
 a. ACEA agreement
 b. ACCRA Cost of Living Index
 c. AD-IA Model
 d. Export

14. In economics, an _____ is any good (e.g. a commodity) or service brought into one country from another country in a legitimate fashion, typically for use in trade. It is a good that is brought in from another country for sale. _____ goods or services are provided to domestic consumers by foreign producers. An _____ in the receiving country is an export to the sending country.
 a. Incoterms
 b. Import quota
 c. Economic integration
 d. Import

15. In finance, the term _____ describes various legal measures taken to ensure that debtors, whether individuals, businesses honor their debts and make an honest effort to repay the money that they owe. Generally regarded as a subdivision of tax law, _____ is most often enforced through a combination of audits and legal restrictions. For example, a provision of the Federal Debt Collection Procedure Act states that a person or organization indebted to the United States, against whom a judgment lien has been filed, is ineligible to receive a government grant.
 a. Microcredit
 b. Carryback loan
 c. Hard money loan
 d. Debt compliance

16. The balance of trade (or net exports, sometimes symbolized as NX) is the difference between the monetary value of exports and imports in an economy over a certain period of time. It is the relationship between a nation's imports and exports. A favorable balance of trade is known as a trade surplus and consists of exporting more than is imported; an unfavorable balance of trade is known as a _____ or, informally, a trade gap.
 a. Demographics of India
 b. Computational economic
 c. Complementary asset
 d. Trade deficit

17. In economics, the _____ measures the payments that flow between any individual country and all other countries. It is used to summarize all international economic transactions for that country during a specific time period, usually a year. The _____ is determined by the country's exports and imports of goods, services, and financial capital, as well as financial transfers.
 a. Gross domestic product per barrel
 b. Gross world product
 c. Skyscraper Index
 d. Balance of payments

Chapter 19. NATIONAL POLICIES AND INTERNATIONAL EXCHANGE

18. A _____ is the transfer of wealth from one party (such as a person or company) to another. A _____ is usually made in exchange for the provision of goods, services or both, or to fulfill a legal obligation.

The simplest and oldest form of _____ is barter, the exchange of one good or service for another.

a. Soft count
b. Payment
c. Going concern
d. Social gravity

19. The _____ is the central banking system of the United States. Created in 1913 by the enactment of the Federal Reserve Act (signed by Woodrow Wilson), it is a quasi-public and quasi-private (government entity with private components) banking system that comprises (1) the presidentially appointed Board of Governors of the _____ in Washington, D.C.; (2) the Federal Open Market Committee; (3) twelve regional Federal Reserve Banks located in major cities throughout the nation acting as fiscal agents for the U.S. Treasury, each with its own nine-member board of directors; (4) numerous other private U.S. member banks, which subscribe to required amounts of non-transferable stock in their regional Federal Reserve Banks; and (5) various advisory councils. Since February 2006, Ben Bernanke has served as the Chairman of the Board of Governors of the _____.

a. Term auction facility
b. Monetary Policy Report to the Congress
c. Federal Reserve System
d. Federal Reserve System Open Market Account

20. In economics, the _____ is that part of the economy which is both run for private profit and is not controlled by the state. By contrast, enterprises that are part of the state are part of the public sector; private, non-profit organizations are regarded as part of the voluntary sector.

A variety of legal structures exist for _____ business organizations, depending on the jurisdiction in which they have their legal domicile.

a. Primary products
b. Secondary sector of the economy
c. Private sector
d. Standard Industrial Classification

21. The _____ is the part of economic and administrative life that deals with the delivery of goods and services by and for the government, whether national, regional or local/municipal.

Examples of _____ activity range from delivering social security, administering urban planning and organising national defenses.

Chapter 19. NATIONAL POLICIES AND INTERNATIONAL EXCHANGE

The organization of the _____ can take several forms, including:

- Direct administration funded through taxation; the delivering organization generally has no specific requirement to meet commercial success criteria, and production decisions are determined by government.
- Publicly owned corporations (in some contexts, especially manufacturing, 'state-owned enterprises'); which differ from direct administration in that they have greater commercial freedoms and are expected to operate according to commercial criteria, and production decisions are not generally taken by government (although goals may be set for them by government.)
- Partial outsourcing (of the scale many businesses do, e.g. for IT services), is considered a _____ model.

A borderline form is

- Complete outsourcing or contracting out, with a privately owned corporation delivering the entire service on behalf of government. This may be considered a mixture of private sector operations with public ownership of assets, although in some forms the private sector's control and/or risk is so great that the service may no longer be considered part of the _____.

a. Policy cycle
b. 130-30 fund
c. 100-year flood
d. Public sector

22. _____ refers to a business or organization attempting to acquire goods or services to accomplish the goals of the enterprise. Though there are several organizations that attempt to set standards in the _____ process, processes can vary greatly between organizations. Typically the word '_____' is not used interchangeably with the word 'procurement', since procurement typically includes Expediting, Supplier Quality, and Traffic and Logistics (T'L) in addition to _____.

a. Free port
b. Purchasing
c. 130-30 fund
d. 100-year flood

23. _____ is the number of goods/services that can be purchased with a unit of currency. For example, if you had taken one dollar to a store in the 1950s, you would have been able to buy a greater number of items than you would today, indicating that you would have had a greater _____ in the 1950s. Currency can be either a commodity money, like gold or silver, or fiat currency like US dollars.

a. Genuine progress indicator
b. Purchasing power
c. Compliance cost
d. Human Poverty Index

24. The _____ theory uses the long-term equilibrium exchange rate of two currencies to equalize their purchasing power. Developed by Gustav Cassel in 1920, it is based on the law of one price: the theory states that, in ideally efficient markets, identical goods should have only one price.

This purchasing power SEM rate equalizes the purchasing power of different currencies in their home countries for a given basket of goods.

Chapter 19. NATIONAL POLICIES AND INTERNATIONAL EXCHANGE

a. Purchasing power parity
b. Gross national product
c. Measures of national income and output
d. Bureau of Labor Statistics

25. The _____ of monetary management established the rules for commercial and financial relations among the world's major industrial states in the mid 20th Century. The _____ was the first example of a fully negotiated monetary order intended to govern monetary relations among independent nation-states.

Preparing to rebuild the international economic system as World War II was still raging, 730 delegates from all 44 Allied nations gathered at the Mount Washington Hotel in Bretton Woods, New Hampshire, United States, for the United Nations Monetary and Financial Conference.

a. 100-year flood
b. 1921 recession
c. Bretton Woods system
d. 130-30 fund

26. _____ is a term used in economic research and policy debates. As with freedom generally, there are various definitions, but no universally accepted concept of _____. One major approach to _____ comes from the libertarian tradition emphasizing free markets and private property, while another extends the welfare economics study of individual choice, with greater _____ coming from a 'larger' (in some technical sense) set of possible choices.

a. Investment policy
b. International sanctions
c. Economic liberalization
d. Economic Freedom

27. A _____ occurs when an entity spends more money than it takes in. The opposite of a _____ is a budget surplus. Debt is essentially an accumulated flow of deficits.

a. Lump-sum tax
b. Funding body
c. Public Financial Management
d. Budget deficit

28. In finance, the _____s between two currencies specifies how much one currency is worth in terms of the other. It is the value of a foreign natione;s currency in terms of the home natione;s currency. For example an _____ of 102 Japanese yen to the United States dollar means that JPY 102 is worth the same as USD 1.

a. ACEA agreement
b. Interbank market
c. ACCRA Cost of Living Index
d. Exchange rate

29. A _____, sometimes called a pegged exchange rate, is a type of exchange rate regime wherein a currency's value is matched to the value of another single currency or to a basket of other currencies such as gold.

A _____ is usually used to stabilize the value of a currency, vis-a-vis the currency it is pegged to. This facilitates trade and investments between the two countries, and is especially useful for small economies where external trade forms a large part of their GDP.

a. Monetary economics
b. Law of supply
c. Leading indicators
d. Fixed exchange rate

30. A _____ or a flexible exchange rate is a type of exchange rate regime wherein a currency's value is allowed to fluctuate according to the foreign exchange market. A currency that uses a _____ is known as a floating currency. The opposite of a _____ is a fixed exchange rate.

Chapter 19. NATIONAL POLICIES AND INTERNATIONAL EXCHANGE

a. Foreign exchange market
b. Trade Weighted US dollar Index
c. Floating currency
d. Floating exchange rate

31. _____ is a term used in accounting, economics and finance to spread the cost of an asset over the span of several years.

In simple words we can say that _____ is the reduction in the value of an asset due to usage, passage of time, wear and tear, technological outdating or obsolescence, depletion, inadequacy, rot, rust, decay or other such factors.

In accounting, _____ is a term used to describe any method of attributing the historical or purchase cost of an asset across its useful life, roughly corresponding to normal wear and tear.

a. Salvage value
b. Historical cost
c. Depreciation
d. Net income per employee

32. _____, in economics, occurs when assets and/or money rapidly flow out of a country, due to an economic event that disturbs investors and causes them to lower their valuation of the assets in that country, or otherwise to lose confidence in its economic strength. This leads to a disappearance of wealth and is usually accompanied by a sharp drop in the exchange rate of the affected country (depreciation in a variable exchange rate regime, or a forced devaluation in a fixed exchange rate regime.)

This fall is particularly damaging when the capital belongs to the people of the affected country, because not only are the citizens now burdened by the loss of faith in the economy and devaluation of their currency, but probably also their assets have lost much of their nominal value.

a. Capital flight
b. Liquid capital
c. Capital formation
d. Firm-specific infrastructure

33. The _____ is the official currency of 16 of the 27 member states of the European Union (EU.) The states, known collectively as the Eurozone, are Austria, Belgium, Cyprus, Finland, France, Germany, Greece, Ireland, Italy, Luxembourg, Malta, the Netherlands, Portugal, Slovakia, Slovenia, and Spain. The currency is also used in a further five European countries, with and without formal agreements and is consequently used daily by some 327 million Europeans.

a. Equity capital market
b. IRS Code 3401
c. Import and Export Price Indices
d. Euro

34. _____ is a fee paid on borrowed assets. It is the price paid for the use of borrowed money, or, money earned by deposited funds. Assets that are sometimes lent with _____ include money, shares, consumer goods through hire purchase, major assets such as aircraft, and even entire factories in finance lease arrangements.

a. Asset protection
b. Internal debt
c. Insolvency
d. Interest

35. The _____, often referred to by the French term raison d'État, is a country's goals and ambitions whether economic, military, or cultural. The notion is an important one in international relations where pursuit of the _____ is the foundation of the realist school.

Chapter 19. NATIONAL POLICIES AND INTERNATIONAL EXCHANGE

The _____ of a state is multi faceted.

a. 1921 recession
b. 100-year flood
c. National interest
d. 130-30 fund

36. The _____ refers to the 'common well-being' or 'general welfare.' The _____ is central to policy debates, politics, democracy and the nature of government itself. While nearly everyone claims that aiding the common well-being or general welfare is positive, there is little, if any, consensus on what exactly constitutes the _____.

There are different views on how many members of the public must benefit from an action before it can be declared to be in the _____: at one extreme, an action has to benefit every single member of society in order to be truly in the _____; at the other extreme, any action can be in the _____ as long as it benefits some of the population and harms none.

a. Power Elite
b. Second-class citizen
c. Stealth tax
d. Public interest

37. In economics, _____ refers to the ability of a person or a country to produce a particular good at a lower marginal cost and opportunity cost than another person or country. It is the ability to produce a product most efficiently given all the other products that could be produced. It can be contrasted with absolute advantage which refers to the ability of a person or a country to produce a particular good at a lower absolute cost than another.

a. Comparative advantage
b. Hot money
c. Triffin dilemma
d. Gravity model of trade

38. The term _____ was initially coined in 1989 by John Williamson to describe a set of ten specific economic policy prescriptions that he considered should constitute the 'standard' reform package promoted for crisis-wracked developing countries by Washington, DC-based institutions such as the International Monetary Fund (IMF), World Bank and the US Treasury Department.

Subsequently, as Williamson himself has pointed out, the term has come to be used in a different and broader sense, as a synonym for market fundamentalism; in this broader sense, Williamson states, it has been criticized by people such as George Soros and Nobel Laureate Joseph E. Stiglitz. The _____ is also criticized by others such as some Latin American politicians and heterodox economists.

a. Minimum wage
b. Secular basis
c. Permanent income hypothesis
d. Washington consensus

39. _____ in its literal sense is the process of transformation of local or regional phenomena into global ones. It can be described as a process by which the people of the world are unified into a single society and function together.

This process is a combination of economic, technological, sociocultural and political forces.

a. Globalization
b. Global Cosmopolitanism
c. Globally Integrated Enterprise
d. Helsinki Process on Globalisation and Democracy

40. The _____ is an international financial institution that provides financial and technical assistance to developing countries for development programs (e.g. bridges, roads, schools, etc.) with the stated goal of reducing poverty.

The _____ differs from the _____ Group, in that the _____ comprises only two institutions:

- International Bank for Reconstruction and Development (IBRD)
- International Development Association (IDA)

Whereas the latter incorporates these two in addition to three more:

- International Finance Corporation (IFC)
- Multilateral Investment Guarantee Agency (MIGA)
- International Centre for Settlement of Investment Disputes (ICSID)

John Maynard Keynes (right) represented the UK at the conference, and Harry Dexter White represented the US.

The _____ is one of two major financial institutions created as a result of the Bretton Woods Conference in 1944. The International Monetary Fund, a related but separate institution, is the second.

a. World Bank
b. Bank-State-Branch
c. Flow to Equity-Approach
d. Financial costs of the 2003 Iraq War

41. The _____ is an important selective, mainly private, international organization designed by its founders to supervise and liberalize international trade. The organization officially commenced on 1 January 1995, under the Marrakesh Agreement, succeeding the 1947 General Agreement on Tariffs and Trade (GATT.)

The _____ deals with regulation of trade between participating countries; it provides a framework for negotiating and formalising trade agreements, and a dispute resolution process aimed at enforcing participants' adherence to _____ agreements which are signed by representatives of member governments and ratified by their parliaments.

a. Bio-energy village
b. 2009 G-20 London summit protests
c. Backus-Kehoe-Kydland consumption correlation puzzle
d. World Trade Organization

42. _____ is a concept in international development, political economy and international relations and describes the use of conditions attached to a loan, debt relief, bilateral aid or membership of international organizations, typically by the international financial institutions, regional organizations or donor countries.

_____ is typically employed by the International Monetary Fund, the World Bank or a donor country with respect to loans, debt relief and financial aid. Conditionalities may involve relatively uncontroversial requirements to enhance aid effectiveness, such as anti-corruption measures, but they may involve highly controversial ones, such as austerity or the privatization of key public services, which may provoke strong political opposition in the recipient country.

Chapter 19. NATIONAL POLICIES AND INTERNATIONAL EXCHANGE

a. Sector-Wide Approach
b. Participatory rural appraisal
c. Capacity Development
d. Conditionality

43. _____ is any (course of) action deliberately taken (or not taken) to manage human activities with a view to prevent, reduce or mitigate harmful effects on nature and natural resources, and ensuring that man-made changes to the environment do not have harmful effects on humans.

It is useful to consider that _____ comprises two major terms: environment and policy. Environment primarily refers to the ecological (ecosystems) dimension, but can also take account of social (quality of life) dimension and an economic (resource management) dimension.

a. ACEA agreement
b. ACCRA Cost of Living Index
c. AD-IA Model
d. Environmental policy

44. A _____ usually refers to an individual entity seeking a more favorable outcome at the expense of other entities by upsetting an equilibrium to their own favor, only to cause an inevitable retaliation by the other individuals to rebalance the equilibrium, resulting in all participants having an overall less favorable outcome. For example, people may have a tendency to buy increasingly larger, heavier, and often more expensive cars because the additional weight can help make the car safer in a collision with a smaller, lighter car. Thus to keep up with the average vehicle weight for safety's sake, drivers must buy heavier, more expensive, less efficient cars, while safety on the whole does not improve compared to when the average vehicle was lighter.

a. Stylized fact
b. Trailing twelve months
c. Fear factor
d. Race to the bottom

45. _____ is a term used to described a tendency or preference towards a particular perspective, ideology or result, especially when the tendency interferes with the ability to be impartial, unprejudiced, or objective. The term _____ed is used to describe an action, judgment, or other outcome influenced by a prejudged perspective. It is also used to refer to a person or body of people whose actions or judgments exhibit _____.

a. 100-year flood
b. Bias
c. 130-30 fund
d. 1921 recession

46. _____ is subcontracting a process, such as product design or manufacturing, to a third-party company. The decision to outsource is often made in the interest of lowering cost or making better use of time and energy costs, redirecting or conserving energy directed at the competencies of a particular business, or to make more efficient use of land, labor, capital, (information) technology and resources. _____ became part of the business lexicon during the 1980s.

a. Averch-Johnson effect
b. Outsourcing
c. Electronic business
d. Additional Funds Needed

Chapter 20. PROMOTING ECONOMIC GROWTH

1. _____s is the social science that studies the production, distribution, and consumption of goods and services. The term _____s comes from the Ancient Greek oá¼°κονομῖα from oá¼¶κος (oikos, 'house') + vĺŒμος (nomos, 'custom' or 'law'), hence 'rules of the house(hold)'. Current _____ models developed out of the broader field of political economy in the late 19th century, owing to a desire to use an empirical approach more akin to the physical sciences.

   a. Inflation
   b. Energy economics
   c. Opportunity cost
   d. Economic

2. _____ is a term used in economic research and policy debates. As with freedom generally, there are various definitions, but no universally accepted concept of _____. One major approach to _____ comes from the libertarian tradition emphasizing free markets and private property, while another extends the welfare economics study of individual choice, with greater _____ coming from a 'larger' (in some technical sense) set of possible choices.

   a. Investment policy
   b. Economic Freedom
   c. Economic liberalization
   d. International sanctions

3. The _____ is institutions that comprise the World Bank Group. The IBRD is an international organization whose original mission was to finance the reconstruction of nations devastated by World War II. Now, its mission has expanded to fight poverty by means of financing states.

   a. International Development Association
   b. United Nations Monetary and Financial Conference
   c. ACCRA Cost of Living Index
   d. International Bank for Reconstruction and Development

4. The _____ is an international financial institution that provides financial and technical assistance to developing countries for development programs (e.g. bridges, roads, schools, etc.) with the stated goal of reducing poverty.

The _____ differs from the _____ Group, in that the _____ comprises only two institutions:

- International Bank for Reconstruction and Development (IBRD)
- International Development Association (IDA)

Whereas the latter incorporates these two in addition to three more:

- International Finance Corporation (IFC)
- Multilateral Investment Guarantee Agency (MIGA)
- International Centre for Settlement of Investment Disputes (ICSID)

John Maynard Keynes (right) represented the UK at the conference, and Harry Dexter White represented the US.

The _____ is one of two major financial institutions created as a result of the Bretton Woods Conference in 1944. The International Monetary Fund, a related but separate institution, is the second.

   a. Bank-State-Branch
   b. Financial costs of the 2003 Iraq War
   c. Flow to Equity-Approach
   d. World Bank

Chapter 20. PROMOTING ECONOMIC GROWTH

5. An _____ or Ä"conomic system is a system that involves the production, distribution and consumption of goods and services between the entities in a particular society. It is the method used by society to produce and distribute goods and services. The _____ is composed of people and institutions, including their relationships to productive resources, such as through the convention of property.

   a. Intention economy
   b. Indicative planning
   c. Information economy
   d. Economic system

6. In finance, the term _____ describes various legal measures taken to ensure that debtors, whether individuals, businesses honor their debts and make an honest effort to repay the money that they owe. Generally regarded as a subdivision of tax law, _____ is most often enforced through a combination of audits and legal restrictions. For example, a provision of the Federal Debt Collection Procedure Act states that a person or organization indebted to the United States, against whom a judgment lien has been filed, is ineligible to receive a government grant.

   a. Hard money loan
   b. Carryback loan
   c. Microcredit
   d. Debt compliance

7. The _____ is a federation of seven emirates situated in the southeast of the Arabian Peninsula in Southwest Asia on the Persian Gulf, bordering Oman and Saudi Arabia. The seven states, termed emirates, are Abu Dhabi, Dubai, Sharjah, Ajman, Umm al-Quwain, Ras al-Khaimah and Fujairah .

The _____, rich in oil and natural gas, has become highly prosperous after gaining foreign direct investment funding in the 1970s.

   a. ACEA agreement
   b. AD-IA Model
   c. ACCRA Cost of Living Index
   d. United Arab Emirates

8. The _____ or gross domestic income (GDI), a basic measure of an economy's economic performance, is the market value of all final goods and services produced within the borders of a nation in a year. _____ can be defined in three ways, all of which are conceptually identical. First, it is equal to the total expenditures for all final goods and services produced within the country in a stipulated period of time (usually a 365-day year.)

   a. Monopolistic competition
   b. Gross domestic product
   c. Countercyclical
   d. Market structure

9. A variety of measures of national income and output are used in economics to estimate total economic activity in a country or region, including gross domestic product (GDP), _____ , and net national income (NNI.)

There are three main ways of calculating these numbers; the output approach, the income approach and the expenditure approach. In theory, the three must yield the same, because total expenditures on goods and services must equal the total income paid to the producers (GNI), and that must also equal the total value of the output of goods and services (_____.)

   a. Purchasing power parity
   b. Gross world product
   c. Household final consumption expenditure
   d. Gross national product

10. The accounting equation relates assets, _____, and owner's equity:

Chapter 20. PROMOTING ECONOMIC GROWTH

Assets = _____ + Owner's Equity

The accounting equation is the mathematical structure of the balance sheet.

The Australian Accounting Research Foundation defines _____ as: 'future sacrifice of economic benefits that the entity is presently obliged to make to other entities as a result of past transactions and other past events.'

Probably the most accepted accounting definition of liability is the one used by the International Accounting Standards Board (IASB.) The following is a quotation from IFRS Framework:

A liability is a present obligation of the enterprise arising from past events, the settlement of which is expected to result in an outflow from the enterprise of resources embodying economic benefits

-

Regulations as to the recognition of _____ are different all over the world, but are roughly similar to those of the IASB.

a. Liabilities
b. Competition law theory
c. Coase theorem
d. Community property

11. The _____ is the broad group of people in contemporary society who fall socioeconomically between the working class and upper class. This socioeconomic class encompasses the sub-classes of lower middle, middle middle, and upper middle, and includes professionals, highly skilled workers, and management. As in all socioeconomic classes, the _____ is associated with a shared and complex set of cultural values.

a. Middle class
b. 130-30 fund
c. Dominant minority
d. 100-year flood

12. _____ is a misspelled phrase from Latin 'pro capite' phrase meaning per head with pro meaning 'per' or 'for each' and capite meaning 'head.' Both words together equate to the phrase 'for each head.'

It is usually used in the field of statistics to indicate the average per person for any given concern, such as income, crime rate, etc.

It is also used in wills to indicate that each of the named beneficiaries should receive, by devise or bequest, equal shares of the estate. This is in contrast to a per stirpes division, in which each branch of the inheriting family inherits an equal share of the estate.

a. False positive rate
b. Sargan test
c. Per capita
d. Population statistics

13. _____ was a survey conducted by the U.S. Department of Justice to gauge the prevalence of alcohol and illegal drug use among prior arrestees. It was a reformulation of the prior Drug Use Forecasting (DUF) program, focused on five drugs in particular: cocaine, marijuana, methamphetamine, opiates, and PCP.

Chapter 20. PROMOTING ECONOMIC GROWTH

Participants were randomly selected from arrest records in major metropolitan areas; because no personally identifying information is taken from each record chosen, the resulting data can be correlated to arrest rates, but not to the total population of persons charged.

a. ACCRA Cost of Living Index
b. AD-IA Model
c. Arrestee Drug Abuse Monitoring
d. ACEA agreement

14. _____ is sometimes referred to as _____, actually it means Economic Monetary Union.

First ideas of an economic and monetary union in Europe were raised well before establishing the European Communities. For example, already in the League of Nations, Gustav Stresemann asked in 1929 for a European currency (Link) against the background of an increased economic division due to a number of new nation states in Europe after WWI.

a. Exchange rate mechanism
b. European Monetary Union
c. Euro Interbank Offered Rate
d. European Monetary System

15.

_____ was a German philosopher, political economist, historian, political theorist, sociologist, communist and revolutionary credited as the founder of communism.

Marx summarized his approach to history and politics in the opening line of the first chapter of The Communist Manifesto : e;The history of all hitherto existing society is the history of class struggles.e; Marx argued that capitalism, like previous socioeconomic systems, will produce internal tensions which will lead to its destruction. Just as capitalism replaced feudalism, socialism will in its turn replace capitalism and lead to a stateless, classless society which will emerge after a transitional period, the 'dictatorship of the proletariat'.

a. Adam Smith
b. Karl Heinrich Marx
c. Marxism
d. Neo-Gramscianism

16. An economic and _____ is a single market with a common currency. It is to be distinguished from a mere currency union , which does not involve a single market. This is the fifth stage of economic integration.

a. Free trade zone
b. Monetary Union
c. Customs union
d. Commercial invoice

17. _____ was a Scottish moral philosopher and a pioneer of political economy. One of the key figures of the Scottish Enlightenment, Smith is the author of The Theory of Moral Sentiments and An Inquiry into the Nature and Causes of the Wealth of Nations. The latter, usually abbreviated as The Wealth of Nations, is considered his magnum opus and the first modern work of economics.

a. Alan Greenspan
b. Adam Smith
c. Adolph Fischer
d. Adolf Hitler

Chapter 20. PROMOTING ECONOMIC GROWTH

18. _____ is the increase in the amount of the goods and services produced by an economy over time. It is conventionally measured as the percent rate of increase in real gross domestic product, or real GDP. Growth is usually calculated in real terms, i.e. inflation-adjusted terms, in order to net out the effect of inflation on the price of the goods and services produced.
   a. ACEA agreement
   b. ACCRA Cost of Living Index
   c. AD-IA Model
   d. Economic growth

19. In finance, _____ is investment originating from other countries. See Foreign direct investment.
   a. Foreign investment
   b. Preclusive purchasing
   c. Demand side economics
   d. Horizontal merger

20. _____ is a type of risk faced by investors, corporations, and governments. It is a risk that can be understood and managed with proper aforethought and investment.

Broadly, _____ refers to the complications businesses and governments may face as a result of what are commonly referred to as political decisions--or e;any political change that alters the expected outcome and value of a given economic action by changing the probability of achieving business objectives.e; .

   a. Black-Derman-Toy model
   b. Political risk
   c. Capital adequacy ratio
   d. Pull to par

21. _____ is a voluntary transfer of resources from one country to another, given at least partly with the objective of benefiting the recipient country. It may have other functions as well: it may be given as a signal of diplomatic approval, or to strengthen a military ally, to reward a government for behaviour desired by the donor, to extend the donor's cultural influence, to provide infrastructure needed by the donor for resource extraction from the recipient country, or to gain other kinds of commercial access. Humanitarianism and altruism are, nevertheless, significant motivations for the giving of _____.
   a. AD-IA Model
   b. ACEA agreement
   c. ACCRA Cost of Living Index
   d. Aid

22. A _____ occurs when an entity spends more money than it takes in. The opposite of a _____ is a budget surplus. Debt is essentially an accumulated flow of deficits.
   a. Funding body
   b. Lump-sum tax
   c. Public Financial Management
   d. Budget deficit

23. _____ in its literal sense is the process of transformation of local or regional phenomena into global ones. It can be described as a process by which the people of the world are unified into a single society and function together.

This process is a combination of economic, technological, sociocultural and political forces.

   a. Globally Integrated Enterprise
   b. Helsinki Process on Globalisation and Democracy
   c. Global Cosmopolitanism
   d. Globalization

24. _____ refers to the stock of skills and knowledge embodied in the ability to perform labor so as to produce economic value. It is the skills and knowledge gained by a worker through education and experience. Many early economic theories refer to it simply as labor, one of three factors of production, and consider it to be a fungible resource -- homogeneous and easily interchangeable. Other conceptions of labor dispense with these assumptions.

Chapter 20. PROMOTING ECONOMIC GROWTH

a. Law of increasing costs
b. Price theory
c. General equilibrium
d. Human capital

25. _____s (economically referred to as land or raw materials) occur naturally within environments that exist relatively undisturbed by mankind, in a natural form. A _____'s is often characterized by amounts of biodiversity existent in various ecosystems.

Mining, petroleum extraction, fishing, hunting, and forestry are generally considered natural-resource industries.

a. 100-year flood
b. 1921 recession
c. 130-30 fund
d. Natural resource

26. An Inquiry into the Nature and Causes of the _____ is the magnum opus of the Scottish economist Adam Smith. It is a clearly written account of economics at the dawn of the Industrial Revolution, as well as a rhetorical piece written for the generally educated individual of the 18th century - advocating a free market economy as more productive and more beneficial to society.

The work is credited as a watershed in history and economics due to its comprehensive, largely accurate characterization of economic mechanisms that survive in modern economics; and also for its effective use of rhetorical technique, including structuring the work to contrast real world examples of free and fettered markets.

a. The Bell Curve
b. The Rise and Fall of the Great Powers
c. Black Book of Communism
d. Wealth of Nations

27. _____ is a fee paid on borrowed assets. It is the price paid for the use of borrowed money , or, money earned by deposited funds . Assets that are sometimes lent with _____ include money, shares, consumer goods through hire purchase, major assets such as aircraft, and even entire factories in finance lease arrangements.

a. Insolvency
b. Internal debt
c. Asset protection
d. Interest

156 Chapter 20. PROMOTING ECONOMIC GROWTH

28. A _____ is:

- Rewrite _____, in generative grammar and computer science
- Standardization, a formal and widely-accepted statement, fact, definition, or qualification
- Operation, a determinate _____ for performing a mathematical operation and obtaining a certain result (Mathematics, Logic)
    - Unary operation
    - Binary operation
- _____ of inference, a function from sets of formulae to formulae (Mathematics, Logic)
- _____ of thumb, principle with broad application that is not intended to be strictly accurate or reliable for every situation. Also often simply referred to as a _____
- Moral, an atomic element of a moral code for guiding choices in human behavior
- Heuristic, a quantized '_____' which shows a tendency or probability for successful function
- A regulation, as in sports
- A Production _____, as in computer science
- Procedural law, a _____ set governing the application of laws to cases
    - A law, which may informally be called a '_____'
    - A court ruling, a decision by a court
- In the U.S. Government, a regulation mandated by Congress, but written or expanded upon by the Executive Branch.
- Norm (sociology), an informal but widely accepted _____, concept, truth, definition, or qualification (social norms, legal norms, coding norms)
- Norm (philosophy), a kind of sentence or a reason to act, feel or believe
- 'Rulership' is the concept of governance by a government:
    - Military _____, governance by a military body
    - Monastic _____, a collection of precepts that guides the life of monks or nuns in a religious order where the superior holds the place of Christ
- Slide _____

- '_____,' a song by Ayumi Hamasaki
- '_____,' a song by rapper Nas
- '_____s,' an album by the band The Whitest Boy Alive
- _____s: Pyaar Ka Superhit Formula, a 2003 Bollywood film
- ruler, an instrument for measuring lengths
- _____, a component of an astrolabe, circumferator or similar instrument
- The _____s, a bestselling self-help book
- _____ Project (Run Up-to-date Linux Everywhere), a project that aims to use up-to-date Linux software on old PCs
- _____ engine, a software system that helps managing business _____s
- Ja _____, a hip hop artist
    - R.U.L.E., a 2005 greatest hits album by rapper Ja _____
- '_____s,' a KMFDM song

a. Technocracy
b. Demand
c. Procter ' Gamble
d. Rule

Chapter 20. PROMOTING ECONOMIC GROWTH

29. _____ is a term used to collectively describe topics relating to the operations of firms with interests in multiple countries. Such firms are sometimes called multinational corporations. Well known MNCs include fast food companies McDonald's and Yum Brands, vehicle manufacturers such as General Motors and Toyota, consumer electronics companies like Samsung, LG and Sony, and energy companies such as ExxonMobil and BP.

    a. AD-IA Model
    b. ACCRA Cost of Living Index
    c. ACEA agreement
    d. International Business

30. _____ is that which is owed; usually referencing assets owed, but the term can also cover moral obligations and other interactions not requiring money. In the case of assets, _____ is a means of using future purchasing power in the present before a summation has been earned. Some companies and corporations use _____ as a part of their overall corporate finance strategy.

    a. Debenture
    b. Hard money loan
    c. Collateral Management
    d. Debt

31. In economics, the _____ is that part of the economy which is both run for private profit and is not controlled by the state. By contrast, enterprises that are part of the state are part of the public sector; private, non-profit organizations are regarded as part of the voluntary sector.

A variety of legal structures exist for _____ business organizations, depending on the jurisdiction in which they have their legal domicile.

    a. Private sector
    b. Secondary sector of the economy
    c. Standard Industrial Classification
    d. Primary products

32. The _____ is the part of economic and administrative life that deals with the delivery of goods and services by and for the government, whether national, regional or local/municipal.

Examples of _____ activity range from delivering social security, administering urban planning and organising national defenses.

The organization of the _____ can take several forms, including:

- Direct administration funded through taxation; the delivering organization generally has no specific requirement to meet commercial success criteria, and production decisions are determined by government.
- Publicly owned corporations (in some contexts, especially manufacturing, 'state-owned enterprises'); which differ from direct administration in that they have greater commercial freedoms and are expected to operate according to commercial criteria, and production decisions are not generally taken by government (although goals may be set for them by government.)
- Partial outsourcing (of the scale many businesses do, e.g. for IT services), is considered a _____ model.

Chapter 20. PROMOTING ECONOMIC GROWTH

A borderline form is

- Complete outsourcing or contracting out, with a privately owned corporation delivering the entire service on behalf of government. This may be considered a mixture of private sector operations with public ownership of assets, although in some forms the private sector's control and/or risk is so great that the service may no longer be considered part of the _____.

a. Public sector
c. Policy cycle
b. 130-30 fund
d. 100-year flood

33. _____ refers to a business or organization attempting to acquire goods or services to accomplish the goals of the enterprise. Though there are several organizations that attempt to set standards in the _____ process, processes can vary greatly between organizations. Typically the word '_____' is not used interchangeably with the word 'procurement', since procurement typically includes Expediting, Supplier Quality, and Traffic and Logistics (T'L) in addition to _____.

a. 100-year flood
c. Purchasing
b. 130-30 fund
d. Free port

34. _____ is the number of goods/services that can be purchased with a unit of currency. For example, if you had taken one dollar to a store in the 1950s, you would have been able to buy a greater number of items than you would today, indicating that you would have had a greater _____ in the 1950s. Currency can be either a commodity money, like gold or silver, or fiat currency like US dollars.

a. Compliance cost
c. Human Poverty Index
b. Genuine progress indicator
d. Purchasing power

35. The _____ theory uses the long-term equilibrium exchange rate of two currencies to equalize their purchasing power. Developed by Gustav Cassel in 1920, it is based on the law of one price: the theory states that, in ideally efficient markets, identical goods should have only one price.

This purchasing power SEM rate equalizes the purchasing power of different currencies in their home countries for a given basket of goods.

a. Purchasing power parity
c. Gross national product
b. Measures of national income and output
d. Bureau of Labor Statistics

Chapter 21. THE LIMITATIONS OF ECONOMICS

1. _____s is the social science that studies the production, distribution, and consumption of goods and services. The term _____s comes from the Ancient Greek oá¼°κονομῖα from oá¼¶κος (oikos, 'house') + vÏŒμος (nomos, 'custom' or 'law'), hence 'rules of the house(hold)'. Current _____ models developed out of the broader field of political economy in the late 19th century, owing to a desire to use an empirical approach more akin to the physical sciences.
    a. Opportunity cost
    b. Inflation
    c. Energy economics
    d. Economic

2. _____ is a term used in economic research and policy debates. As with freedom generally, there are various definitions, but no universally accepted concept of _____. One major approach to _____ comes from the libertarian tradition emphasizing free markets and private property, while another extends the welfare economics study of individual choice, with greater _____ coming from a 'larger' (in some technical sense) set of possible choices.
    a. Economic liberalization
    b. International sanctions
    c. Investment policy
    d. Economic Freedom

3. _____, or a _____ is the concept of a resulting effect (cf. cause and effect, arising from another action. In general terms, it is used to indicate that all human actions, particularly crime and sin, have profound effects.
    a. Rule
    b. Consequence
    c. Solved
    d. Variability

4. _____ was a survey conducted by the U.S. Department of Justice to gauge the prevalence of alcohol and illegal drug use among prior arrestees. It was a reformulation of the prior Drug Use Forecasting (DUF) program, focused on five drugs in particular: cocaine, marijuana, methamphetamine, opiates, and PCP.

Participants were randomly selected from arrest records in major metropolitan areas; because no personally identifying information is taken from each record chosen, the resulting data can be correlated to arrest rates, but not to the total population of persons charged.

    a. Arrestee Drug Abuse Monitoring
    b. ACCRA Cost of Living Index
    c. AD-IA Model
    d. ACEA agreement

5. _____ was a Scottish moral philosopher and a pioneer of political economy. One of the key figures of the Scottish Enlightenment, Smith is the author of The Theory of Moral Sentiments and An Inquiry into the Nature and Causes of the Wealth of Nations. The latter, usually abbreviated as The Wealth of Nations, is considered his magnum opus and the first modern work of economics.
    a. Adolph Fischer
    b. Adam Smith
    c. Alan Greenspan
    d. Adolf Hitler

6. The _____ was written by Adam Smith in 1759. It provided the ethical, philosophical, psychological and methodological underpinnings to Smith's later works, including The Wealth of Nations (1776), A Treatise on Public Opulence (1764) (first published in 1937), Essays on Philosophical Subjects (1795), and Lectures on Justice, Police, Revenue, and Arms (1763) (first published in 1896.)

Broadly speaking, Smith followed the views of his mentor, Francis Hutcheson of the University of Glasgow, who divided moral philosophy into four parts: Ethics and Virtue; Private rights and Natural liberty; Familial rights (called Economics); and State and Individual rights (called Politics.)

Chapter 21. THE LIMITATIONS OF ECONOMICS

a. Capital and Interest
b. Butterfly Economics
c. Limits to Growth
d. Theory of Moral Sentiments

7. _____, 1st Baron Keynes was a renowned economist from Britain whose many ideas on economic and political theories as well as on many governments' monetary policies influenced America. He advocated a government that played an active role in the lives of people regarding business, economy, etc. In this role, the government would use fiscal measures to reduce the consequences of recessions, economic depressions and booms.

a. Adam Smith
b. John Maynard Keynes
c. Adolf Hitler
d. Adolph Fischer

ANSWER KEY

Chapter 1
1. b 2. d 3. c 4. b 5. b 6. d 7. d 8. d 9. c 10. c
11. d 12. d 13. a 14. d 15. d 16. d 17. d 18. d 19. d 20. d
21. a 22. b 23. c 24. b 25. a 26. a 27. a 28. d

Chapter 2
1. d 2. c 3. b 4. a 5. d 6. d 7. d 8. d 9. c 10. c
11. c 12. b 13. d 14. d 15. c 16. d 17. d 18. a 19. d 20. b
21. d 22. b 23. d 24. d 25. a 26. b 27. c 28. d 29. d 30. d
31. d 32. b 33. d 34. d 35. a 36. c 37. b 38. c 39. d 40. d
41. d 42. d 43. d

Chapter 3
1. b 2. d 3. d 4. d 5. b 6. a 7. a 8. d 9. d 10. b
11. b 12. d 13. c 14. b 15. d 16. d 17. c 18. b 19. a 20. b
21. d 22. a 23. d 24. b 25. d 26. d 27. c 28. b 29. c 30. d
31. d 32. c 33. c 34. a

Chapter 4
1. a 2. d 3. d 4. b 5. c 6. d 7. a 8. d 9. d 10. d
11. d 12. b 13. d 14. d

Chapter 5
1. d 2. d 3. d 4. d 5. d 6. d 7. c 8. a 9. b 10. c
11. a 12. d 13. c 14. d 15. a 16. a 17. d 18. b 19. d 20. d
21. b 22. b 23. d 24. d 25. b 26. d 27. d 28. b 29. a 30. c
31. d 32. b 33. d 34. d 35. b 36. d 37. d 38. a 39. b 40. b
41. d 42. c 43. a 44. d

Chapter 6
1. a 2. a 3. b 4. b 5. d 6. a 7. c 8. d 9. d 10. d
11. d 12. b 13. d 14. a 15. b 16. d 17. d 18. d 19. d 20. d
21. d 22. d 23. d 24. d 25. d 26. b 27. d 28. d 29. b 30. b
31. d 32. d 33. d 34. d 35. d 36. c 37. b 38. d 39. c 40. c

Chapter 7
1. b 2. d 3. d 4. d 5. d 6. d 7. d 8. b 9. d 10. d
11. d 12. d 13. d 14. a 15. c 16. c 17. a 18. b 19. c 20. d
21. d 22. b 23. d 24. b 25. c 26. d 27. b 28. d 29. a 30. a
31. a 32. d 33. b 34. b 35. c 36. d 37. c 38. d 39. a 40. b
41. c 42. b 43. d 44. b 45. c 46. a 47. d 48. a 49. d 50. d
51. d 52. b 53. d 54. d 55. d 56. d 57. d 58. d 59. c 60. d
61. d 62. d 63. d 64. d 65. a 66. b 67. a 68. b

ANSWER KEY

Chapter 8
1. c   2. b   3. b   4. b   5. d   6. d   7. d   8. a   9. c   10. d
11. d   12. d   13. d   14. d   15. a   16. d   17. a   18. a   19. d   20. a

Chapter 9
1. d   2. d   3. d   4. c   5. b   6. d   7. d   8. d   9. d   10. d
11. d   12. d   13. a   14. d   15. c   16. d

Chapter 10
1. b   2. d   3. b   4. d   5. a   6. d   7. b   8. d   9. d   10. d
11. c   12. b   13. b   14. b   15. b   16. c   17. d   18. d   19. a   20. d
21. c   22. d   23. d   24. b   25. d   26. d   27. d   28. d   29. b   30. b
31. d   32. c   33. d   34. c   35. b   36. b

Chapter 11
1. d   2. c   3. a   4. c   5. b   6. a   7. b   8. b   9. d   10. d
11. d   12. a   13. d   14. c   15. d   16. a   17. a   18. d   19. a   20. b
21. b   22. a   23. d   24. d   25. c   26. d   27. d   28. b   29. d   30. c
31. d   32. d   33. c   34. a   35. d

Chapter 12
1. a   2. a   3. d   4. d   5. c   6. c   7. d   8. d   9. d   10. d
11. d   12. d   13. b   14. b   15. a   16. c   17. d   18. d   19. d   20. c
21. a   22. b   23. d   24. c   25. c   26. b

Chapter 13
1. a   2. d   3. a   4. d   5. a   6. d   7. a   8. d   9. d   10. d
11. d   12. d   13. d   14. d   15. a   16. d   17. c   18. d   19. d   20. a
21. b   22. d   23. d   24. b   25. a   26. a   27. c

Chapter 14
1. d   2. d   3. d   4. d   5. b   6. b   7. d   8. a   9. d   10. d
11. b   12. a   13. d   14. d   15. d   16. d   17. d   18. d   19. a   20. d
21. d   22. d   23. b   24. d   25. d   26. b   27. c   28. d   29. a   30. c
31. b   32. d   33. a   34. d   35. a   36. a   37. b   38. b   39. b   40. d
41. a   42. d   43. d   44. a

Chapter 15
1. a   2. d   3. d   4. b   5. c   6. d   7. a   8. a   9. d   10. d
11. c   12. d   13. d   14. d   15. d   16. d   17. b   18. d   19. d   20. a
21. d   22. d   23. c   24. a   25. d   26. d   27. a   28. d

ANSWER KEY

Chapter 16

1. b	2. d	3. c	4. b	5. b	6. b	7. d	8. d	9. a	10. d
11. d	12. d	13. d	14. d	15. d	16. b	17. d	18. d	19. d	20. d
21. d	22. d	23. d	24. d	25. a	26. d	27. c	28. a	29. d	30. d

Chapter 17

1. d	2. b	3. d	4. d	5. c	6. d	7. c	8. c	9. c	10. d
11. d	12. d	13. b	14. a	15. d	16. d	17. d	18. d	19. c	20. d
21. d	22. d	23. c	24. d	25. c	26. d	27. c	28. a	29. c	30. d
31. d	32. b	33. c	34. b	35. b	36. b	37. c	38. c	39. d	40. c
41. d	42. c	43. b	44. c	45. c					

Chapter 18

1. a	2. a	3. d	4. a	5. b	6. d	7. a	8. d	9. b	10. d
11. d	12. c	13. c	14. b	15. d	16. b	17. a	18. d	19. c	20. a
21. a	22. a	23. a	24. d	25. c	26. d	27. c	28. c	29. d	30. d
31. d	32. b	33. d	34. d	35. a	36. c	37. d			

Chapter 19

1. b	2. d	3. d	4. c	5. d	6. d	7. c	8. d	9. d	10. d
11. c	12. b	13. d	14. d	15. d	16. d	17. d	18. b	19. c	20. c
21. d	22. b	23. b	24. a	25. c	26. d	27. d	28. d	29. d	30. d
31. c	32. a	33. d	34. d	35. c	36. d	37. a	38. d	39. a	40. a
41. d	42. d	43. d	44. d	45. b	46. b				

Chapter 20

1. d	2. b	3. d	4. d	5. d	6. d	7. d	8. b	9. d	10. a
11. a	12. c	13. c	14. b	15. b	16. b	17. b	18. d	19. a	20. b
21. d	22. d	23. d	24. d	25. d	26. d	27. d	28. d	29. d	30. d
31. a	32. a	33. c	34. d	35. a					

Chapter 21

| 1. d | 2. d | 3. b | 4. a | 5. b | 6. d | 7. b |

www.ingramcontent.com/pod-product-compliance
Lightning Source LLC
Chambersburg PA
CBHW082204230426
43672CB00015B/2896